Don't forget to check out the excellent resources on the Companion Website for your text - www.ablongman.com/smith5e!

Go to the Companion Website for *Introduction to Special Education: Teaching in an Age of Opportunity, 5/e.* With chapter-by-chapter resources the website is a valuable resource to help you learn more about special education.

With the Companion Website, you can:

Learn More about the Classroom – features digitized classroom video footage and interviews with students and special education teachers.

Extend your Learning – there are many activities (including matching, labeling and web activities) on the website that ask you to apply what you have learnt in each chapter.

Includes a printable grid correlating your textbook with the Praxis II exam and INTASC and CEC standards.

Study for Tests - *Practice Test questions* allow you to assess your understanding of each chapter by answering multiple-choice, true/false and essay questions.

Learn more about the history of special education - the website also features an interactive Special Education Timeline that highlights the people and events that have shaped special education through history.

Research and review *New York Times* **articles** – the eThemes of the Times section of the website features over 25 specially selected articles from the *New York Times* archives on special education topics. Each article features critical thinking questions to increase your understanding.

Study Guide for

Smith

Introduction to
Special Education

Teaching in an Age of Opportunity

Fifth Edition

prepared by

Deborah Deutsch Smith
Vanderbilt University

Naomi Chowdhuri Tyler
Vanderbilt University

Susan Saunders Flippin
Vanderbilt University

Boston   New York   San Francisco
Mexico City   Montreal   Toronto   London   Madrid   Munich   Paris
Hong Kong   Singapore   Tokyo   Cape Town   Sydney

TABLE OF CONTENTS

TO THE STUDENT

TO THE STUDENT

This *Study Guide* (SG) was prepared to provide a road map through each of the chapters in the textbook. Although the units in this manual will not give you all of the answers to your questions about individuals with disabilities and exceptionalities, they may, at least, provide a listing of some of the salient and important features of each chapter. In addition, each unit may give you a structure that parallels the exams for your course.

Different sections of the SG were designed for you to test your understanding of the concepts presented in the text. At the end of this manual you will find sample test questions, including types often found in quizzes, midterms, and final examinations. For the multiple choice questions, immediate feedback is available from an answer key. A number of short answer, open-ended questions help you think beyond the concepts presented.

Working with individuals with special needs is challenging and demanding. As a practitioner, you will be required to make decisions based not only on your formal knowledge, but also on your ability to think divergently and solve problems thoughtfully. Books and the Internet may give you some answers, but your ability to think and hypothesize well is the key to successful learning. We hope the wide-range of activities included in this SG will help you begin that process.

Using this manual along with the textbook means that you must interact actively with the material. Just sitting down and filling in the answers without thinking about them is a waste of your time. It is important to feel motivated to learn the material, and to use that motivation to study actively. It is also important to have a positive attitude that says, "I know I'll do well because I know how to study and learn." Current research has repeatedly shown that when students make positive comments or attributions to themselves about their abilities, they score significantly better on tests, perform better in athletics, and in other situations as well. It is a proven fact: believing in your own abilities can make a difference.

Have you ever heard the expression, "Don't work harder, work smarter?" The first section of this SG, written by Diane Shaner Bassett, provides you with a variety of tools to help you work smarter. Read the first section of the SG carefully. It was created to help you study more efficiently and effectively. The tips provided can be applied to all of your studies, and brings you strategies and techniques that are proven through research to help students master and remember content presented at school.

In the next section of the SG you will find units of activities that correspond to each chapter in the textbook. The units have many purposes. First, they provide an overview of the important points covered in each chapter. Second, they integrate content. Third, they further develop your special education vocabulary. Fourth, these units posit problems for you to solve based on your newly acquired knowledge in the area, and they require you to actively manipulate the information you are learning. Each unit includes different types of activities, which are described below. Take a moment to read through the descriptions, so that you can match your learning style to the different parts of the units.

I. *Important points to remember.* These points will help you understand the salient issues and concepts of each chapter. When being evaluated, you should be able to explain in greater detail each of these general statements.

II. *Timeline.* Brief timelines are found in every unit. They give you a linear, visual map of the origins of that particular exceptionality or field of special education. They are organized to help you to remember important dates, names, and events.

III. *Main ideas and details.* The notetaking section in the opening chapter of this manual describes how to take notes efficiently using a two-column format. In the left-hand column, main ideas are to be written; in the right-hand column specific details are to be identified. This format is included, already partially filled in, in each unit. You can use the main ideas and details to aid your notetaking, or to check yourself to be sure you have taken thorough notes during class. Space is provided for you to fill in extra topics and details.

IV. *Define these terms.* This section lists the key words or terms important to the chapter. You should be able to understand them so you can define them in your own words. If you get stuck, you can use the glossary at the back of the text to help you out.

V. *Alphabet soup.* The field of special education is filled with abbreviations or acronyms which represent commonly used key terms, words, or phrases. To become familiar with these terms (which you will use many times in your professional career), this section asks that you learn both the abbreviation, and the term it stands for.

VI. *Study organizers.* This section is a compilation of the main concepts offered in the chapter. It provides a number of different strategies or techniques to help you gain mastery of the material. These techniques include mnemonics, webs, visuals, charts, and outlines. You may use this section to aid in memorization, to recall specific points to remember some important people, or to get a broader view of the concepts.

VII. *Web activities.* In each chapter, you will find two activities that require use of the Internet. The sites we have given you are only starting places for what we hope will lead to fun-explorations.

VIII. *Focus questions.* This section restates the questions found at the beginning of each chapter in the textbook. You should be able to answer these questions. If not, go back and review those concepts you are not yet comfortable with. Remember, these questions are answered in the summary sections at the end of the text chapters.

IX. *Thinking about dilemmas to solve.* These questions pose current dilemmas in the field. They are meant to help you think about issues students with disabilities face.

X. *Putting it all together.* At last you are ready to put this knowledge to good use! This section will help you directly prepare for your exam. Some units also include mini-case studies where you can apply your knowledge to an actual case of an individual with a disability. There are sections in each unit which include concepts to be memorized, problem solving, and recall of information. Briefly, they include (1) *Discussion Questions* - to help you prepare for essays based on facts and concepts, and (2) *Mini-Case Study* (beginning in Chapter 3).

XI. *Puzzles: A time to play.* These games are a fun way to see if you know terms, history, and facts.

XII. *Making Connections.* This section provides a self- exploration activity to help expand your knowledge base beyond what you have learned in the textbook.

We hope the SG makes your learning easier and more fun. To all of you, our best for a great academic term.

DEDICATION

To:

Jim, Steve, and The Little Red Hen	Ken, Kyra, Kailyn and Winnie-the-Pooh	Houston and Melinda

ACKNOWLEDGMENTS

Preparing the *Study Guide* provided us with the opportunity to translate research into practice, to develop activities which should help students of any age learn and remember important content, and to see if a product can be developed that improves upon those which came before it. Also, this project was such a pleasure because of the wonderful people who worked with us and so generously gave of their expertise and talents to make this resource manual practical, usable, and interesting. To all of you who helped, across editions, in so many ways, thanks.

Special gratitude is owed to some very dear and uniquely talented people. Diane Shaner Bassett wrote the introductory chapter. We are confident that students using this manual will be able to study more effectively and efficiently because of her excellent synthesis of the research on study skills and her translation of that research into practical and usable tips. Mary Ann Zipperich introduced us to the concept of webbing found in this Study Guide. Chris Curran created some of the case studies. We also thank Virginia Lanigan for allowing us the freedom to be creative in the fairly uncreative world of study guides. We thank Katherine Falk, who drew the wonderful pictorial mnemonic about Alan in Chapter 1.

DDS
NCT
SSF

STUDYING MORE EFFICIENTLY AND EFFECTIVELY
by
Diane Shaner Bassett

It is important to realize that study skills are not just something one does to prepare for an exam, they are part of a process that starts long before the material to be studied is ever presented. To help you get organized for efficient studying, I divided the acquisition of study skills into three distinct areas: the **Before Stage** which includes time and organizational management techniques; the **During Stage** which includes strategies for listening, notetaking, reading, and using the study units found in this guide; and the **After Stage** which features strategies for taking tests and self-management. By using this process, you can see that taking an exam is just one small part of learning.

BEFORE

Time and Organizational Management

Many times, good time management skills do more to improve your grades than knowing the actual content of the course. Using time effectively means that you are in control of how you want to organize your life. How many times do we say we will have enough time to do some task, only to find that time has slipped away? Unfortunately, time cannot be renewed. It is a resource that must be carefully managed.

Many students feel they need huge blocks of time to study effectively. It is easy to procrastinate, thinking, "I'll have all tomorrow to write this paper." However, true time management relies on the effective use of both large and small parcels of time. In fact, small, frequent snatches of time can be most effective for reviews before a test. By planning a study schedule, you will have a better idea about where and how to get started. You will be less likely to procrastinate, knowing you have set aside a reasonable amount of time to study. This, of course, will provide you with guilt-free time to do the things you really enjoy!

Again, studying is best accomplished as a process. There are times when it is more effective to study for longer sessions, with periodic short breaks built into your schedule. A quick 15-minute review after a lecture class or before a discussion session will double your retention of the material presented. Instead of cramming for a test the night before, segment your studying into daily half hour-blocks. That way, the material will not seem so overwhelming. You will also find that you can synthesize what you have learned better because you have allowed yourself the time to reflect on your learning.

The following tips are offered as suggestions to help you better manage your study time. If you can incorporate just one of these techniques each week, you will surely be a more effective manager of time.

1. *Plan two hours of study time for each hour you spend in class.* This means that if you are taking a 12 hour load, you should plan to spend 24 hours a week to study. That works out to roughly four hours a day, with a day off to relax.

2. *Allocate a definite period of time each day to study.* Make an appointment with yourself to study! That way, you will avoid the Procrastination Syndrome, and have free time to spend on other activities.

3. *Try to find the best time of day for you to study.* Although many of us consider ourselves night owls, studying is actually more efficient if done during the day. Even though you may have school or job commitments during the day, see if there is a block of time appropriate for studying. If you must study at night, set yourself a reasonable "stopping time." This will keep you more alert and effective during your studying time, and will also help you function better the next day.

4. *Study difficult or boring subjects first.* Use your brain power at its freshest to study the subjects confounding you first. Although most people find it more appealing to study the things they like first, you may find it more difficult to concentrate when you reach the harder subjects. By studying your least favorite or hardest courses first, the rest of your studying will come more easily and you might be done studying sooner.

5.   *Study in short blocks of time.* Instead of "pulling an all-nighter" or trying to study everything in one day, limit your studying to no more than three hours at a time. Within the three-hour period, study for fifty minutes and then take a ten-minute break. Use your break to stretch, walk around, or grab something to eat or drink. You can also find wonderful times to study in short intervals. For example, if you have a dental appointment, take notecards or 1 or 2 pages of study notes with you (do not overdo bringing your notes - it will seem overwhelming). Use this quiet time to quickly review a specific part of your course.

6.   *Find a consistent place to study.* Make sure there is somewhere in your dorm room, apartment, or house where you can spread your things around, where there are no distractions. Libraries are good study areas because there are no phones to distract you, and you might get more done in a shorter period of time. Computer pods can be most effective because most people are there for a limited time only. Do not sprawl across your couch; you may discover a quick two hours have passed in napping. Good lighting and ventilation help keep you alert and thinking.

7.   *Collect all the materials you will need before studying.* If all of your books, notes, and papers are gathered in one place, it lessens the chance of becoming distracted while you look for them in other places. Get seated and stay there for awhile!

8.   *Use the "swiss cheese" approach to tackling a large task.* Huge assignments often seem overwhelming in scope. You can help minimize your anxiety by tackling a huge project by punching holes or "swiss cheesing" it. In other words, every day tackle a piece of a project; you will find that completing the little pieces result in substantial chunks of the work to be done, and eventually result in the total task being completed. Using this approach, even large projects do not seem so overwhelming.

9.   *Stay off the telephone.* If you are studying at home, nothing can eat up your time more than a series of short (or long) phone calls. They disrupt your train of thought and take up more time than you realize. Have someone else take messages, get an answering machine, or take

the phone off the hook. Better yet, go to the library, find a good study carrel out of the mainstream, and use your time wisely.

10. *Use metacognitive strategies.* Just as you think about the content of your studying, think about how you are doing while you are studying. Ask yourself, "Do I have everything I need? Am I concentrating? Am I working hard so I can take a nice 10 minute break? What have I just learned?" By focusing on the process of **how** you are studying **while** you are studying, you can keep tabs on your effectiveness and on your time limitations as well.

Time and organization can be your best allies or your worst enemies. These two factors are, however, well within your control if you exercise some good judgment and thoughtful planning. Use the above strategies to make it easier on yourself.

DURING

The **During Stage** represents those areas of study which are utilized during the acquisition of the content or material. Within each of these areas are specific skills and strategies which can be employed to enhance both the acquisition and retention of course material and information. These areas include listening strategies, notetaking strategies, and reading strategies. In addition, we have added a section that explains the various techniques utilized in the units which follow this chapter. The units are organized in similar formats. You can study and take practice tests within each chapter. Please note also that a couple of the study units employ specific study strategies like **webbing** (an outlining method) and **pictorial mnemonics** (a strategy to help visualize the components of what you are studying by linking them together in a visual way).

Listening and Notetaking Strategies

All of us have spent a substantial part of our school careers listening to instructors and taking notes on what was presented. Some of us do this efficiently, while others have great difficulty. Some practitioners have found that people spend 45% of their day engaged in listening, 30% of the day speaking, 16% of the day reading, and 9% of the day writing. Even with

4

such a high percentage of time devoted to listening, they estimate that people listen with only 25% accuracy.

What can be done to improve this? The following strategies may help you become a better listener in class.

1. *Take an active role in listening.* It sounds funny, but listening is work if you take an active role. Your heart beats faster, your blood circulates more quickly, and your body temperature rises slightly. When listening to a speaker, sit close to the front of the room, sit up in your seat, maintain good eye contact, and respond nonverbally to the speaker by nodding, smiling, or acknowledging what has been said. Participate in class activities by asking questions, volunteering for demonstrations, and taking part in discussions.

2. Concentrate on the content, not the style of delivery. It is very easy to sit and analyze instructors' delivery styles, down to what they are wearing and what kind of accent is used. However, such analysis detracts from the content presented. Do not allow your judgment and attitudes about a speaker's attire, voice, or manner of delivery mask the information given. You may miss many important points.

3. *Be alert to clues and key words in delivery.* Instructors' actions may emphasize the key elements of a lecture or presentation. They may **repeat** certain words or phrases for emphasis. They may **preface** pertinent remarks with phrases such as "for example," "most importantly," or "on the other hand." Use these clues to help highlight important material gathered into your notes.

4. *Be aware of nonverbal clues.* Listening includes an awareness of nonverbal clues instructors give. Are they excited about this portion of the lecture? Are they pointing to a statement for emphasis? Is a key term written on the board? Is the instructor speaking more slowly and methodically so everyone understands the point or concept presented? Both body language and voice inflection and tone can give you important clues to what instructors deem important.

5. *Allow daydreaming to help you refocus.* All of us find ourselves daydreaming. The trick is to use the daydreaming to help you to refocus back to the instructor. Instead of berating yourself for your

daydreaming, use it as a tool to help strengthen your attending powers. Say to yourself, "I can pull myself back clearly to what is happening now."

Notetaking can be the most effective tool you will use, provided you take those notes effectively. Good notes come from a structure and format which lend themselves to easy retrieval later. It has little to do with how fast you can write or how legible your handwriting is; rather, well-organized and concise notes can provide a map for future studying. Here are some strategies for successful notetaking.

1. *Use either a three-ring binder or spiral notebook for each course.* If you like to take all of your notes and spread them out in front of you, use a three-ring binder. If you would rather keep the pages intact, use a spiral notebook. Whether you use a binder or notebook, be sure there is a pocket or a way to add in handouts. Also, write on only the front page of each sheet. This makes notetaking less awkward, and many people pay less attention to the back side of pages. Also, you can see all of your notes if you spread them out.

2. *Put the date and title of the lecture at the beginning of your notetaking.* By marking your notes in this manner, you can compare them back to the course syllabus, and with others in a study group. Also, your notes will stay in order better if you spread them out when studying.

3. *Use the Cornell system of notetaking.* Draw a vertical line from the top to the bottom about 2 inches from the left side of the paper. Use the right side of the paper to record your notes. Use the left side to write in main ideas and key words. You can also add symbols in the left hand column to indicate questions, key points, and vocabulary. Some people even use different colored pens or highlighters to emphasize specific points.

4. *Devise a symbol to indicate you were lost or left something out.* Sometimes we find ourselves daydreaming and when we refocus, we have missed a whole section of notes. When this happens, devise a symbol to put into your notes, indicating that you will contact either your instructor or a fellow student for clarification later. This symbol

will help you remember to complete your notes before you start to study.

5.   *Use "white space" effectively.* Do not try to cram all your notes into one page with tiny handwriting. Leaving "white" or blank spaces on the paper can be visually restful to your eyes and can enable you to focus on the important elements. Later, while studying, you can use the white space for further comments, visuals, or mnemonic clues.

Good notetaking is only as effective as the way in which the notes are used. Plan to review your notes within 24 hours of taking them, and afterwards on a daily basis. Use those 10 to 15 minute waits for class or a bus to do quick reviews of a particular section. Highlight or organize with graphic symbols those concepts or facts you think are important. As your notetaking competence grows, you will find that your notes are more complete and useful, and you will probably want to refine or redo the notes you took earlier in the semester or quarter.

Reading Strategies

It is virtually impossible to go through a day without reading something like a newspaper, magazine, a book, or the mail. However, reading a newspaper is very different from gleaning information from a textbook. Reading for meaning and information from textbooks can be much more difficult, tedious, and challenging to every reader. Therefore, it is important to arm yourself with many strategies to help you absorb the material as quickly and efficiently as possible.

Many readers think that all there is to reading is just reading. They do not realize that reading is a process. Some strategies applied before reading the text help to gain an overview of the material presented. Some strategies used **while** reading the material help you organize and understand the information presented, while others employed **after** reading help you clarify and retain the information. Use your reading skills with the next section to discover how to improve your reading rate and comprehension.

1.   *Use THRILD before you read.* When assigned a chapter or an article, do not just start reading. Instead, give the material a quick, five minute look. Mnemonics are learning strategies developed to help

students learn and remember content presented at school. They are discussed, and some examples given, in Chapter 4: Learning Disabilities of your text. The mnemonic **THRILD** was developed to help you through the steps of the overview process. (To remember the name of this mnemonic, think about how thrilled you are to have this strategy available to you.)

T	Read **T**itle of chapter or article.
H	Read **H**eadings appearing in each subsection.
R	**R**ead first paragraph or introduction of the text.
I	Look at the **I**llustrations, graphs, and visuals presented.
L	Read **L**ast paragraph or concluding section of the text.
D	Read the **D**iscussion questions (advance organizers) at the beginning and end of the text or in your resource manual.

By allowing yourself five minutes to preview the text, your comprehension of the material will increase dramatically because you have an idea of what will be presented. You have read the study questions beforehand, so as you are reading, you can look for them in the text.

2.   *Determine your reading speed.* It helps to know what your reading speed will be on a particular text when you have planned to study for a specific block of time. Use these guidelines to estimate your speed.

   a. TIME yourself reading the text for six minutes.
   b. COUNT the number of pages you completed within the six minute limit.
   c. MULTIPLY the number of pages you read by ten to determine how many pages you can read in an hour.
   d. DIVIDE the number of pages you can read in an hour <u>into</u> the total number of pages you must read.

3.   *Use the strategy "RAP."* This strategy was designed to improve your comprehension and retention of the material. Researchers at the University of Kansas have developed many specific learning strategies (refer to Chapter 4: Learning Disabilities in your text for more information). One of the strategies was designed to improve comprehension and retention of print materials. Using the mnemonic, **RAP**, students improved their comprehension rates from 48% before

the strategy was used to 84% after the strategy was employed. The steps of RAP are listed below.

   a. **READ** a paragraph or section silently.
   b. **ASK** yourself, "What were the main ideas and details of this paragraph?"
   c. **PUT** the main idea and details in your own words.

This strategy is a paraphrasing strategy. When you put the information into your own words, make sure that it is a complete thought (including subject and verb), it contains accurate and new information, it makes sense, and it is phrased in your own words. You may find that you start slowly with this strategy, but that speed will pick up as the strategy is mastered.

4.   *Plan to use additional strategies when the reading is difficult.* Certain sections of reading material are harder than others. When reading such difficult passages, try the following tips.

   a. Read the passage again the next day, when you are fresh to the information.
   b. Read the passage aloud, adding emphasis where appropriate.
   c. Use your instructor to clarify a point. Many times, there are tutors available through the university system. Use them. They are there for you!
   d. Use an alternate text. Reading the same material from a different author may help to clarify certain points.
   e. Stand up! Walk around while you are reading. It may help to focus your attention.

5.   *Use highlighters to emphasize important points.* Try using different colors to emphasize different points. Be sure, however, not to highlight everything. Stick with the main ideas. You can use your notes for the more specific points. Highlighted text stands out when reviewing the material.

6.   *Use the SSG regularly.* Each unit in the manual was designed to help you learn, understand, and remember the content presented in each chapter of your textbook. Read the chapter in the text first while using the strategies we have just described. At the next study time

you have scheduled for yourself, complete the related unit in the SSG. After your instructor's lecture on this topic, review the unit again and add in the extra information from the lecture. Do not wait until the night before a test to start the unit. By then, it is probably too late! Before a test, it would be useful to review each unit and the notes you have added.

Use these strategies to take control of your reading efficiency. If you look at reading as a process, you will find that it flows more smoothly, and will give you more time for other things. Do it right the first time, and you will find you are using your time more efficiently.

AFTER

Taking Tests

You have been following the course content consistently across the term. You have attended class, read the materials, taken good notes, and reviewed the concepts in smaller, frequent doses. All that is left to do is to evaluate your performance on an examination. You have reached the **After** component of study skills. If you have done everything right up to this point, an examination should prove challenging yet achievable.

Many people approach taking tests like they do getting a shot from the doctor. They avoid thinking about it until the last possible moment. Then they rush in, and get it over with as quickly as possible. There is little thought given as to how to lessen the pain or to control the process. Taking tests does not have to be a painful process. Tests do not have to be formidable objects to hurdle, but rather small hills over which to bounce.

The researchers at the University of Kansas also looked at tests and test behaviors and discovered some interesting concepts. For one thing, many people do not stop to look over the test and invent a way to approach the test logically. They tend to rush through it. Most test takers do not allocate themselves time depending on the length and difficulty of the sections of the test, and many test takers do not go back for a second look to review their answers or complete the items they skipped. Based upon these observations, the researchers developed a test taking strategy.

Components of this strategy, along with other suggestions, are described below.

1. *Read the entire test first, including the instructions.* When you first receive the test, look over the entire test to get a feel for its length and difficulty. Then, you will have a better idea of how to spend your time wisely. Be sure to read through the instructions to see if there are any special requirements.

2. *Complete the easier questions first.* Although you were told to study your harder subjects first, answer the easier questions first. This accomplishes several things. It gives you the time to answer what you do know, ensuring at least a partial grade. It also leaves you a block of time to tackle those questions of which you are not so sure. By answering the easier questions first, you will develop a pace and may even find clues to some of the other answers.

3. *On multiple choice questions, employ a number of strategies.* Answer each question in your head before you look at the choices. Determine whether you are to mark one response or more than one. If you have to guess at an answer, try these tips: Eliminate similar answers, avoid absolute words like always and never; choose the most detailed answer; if two answers are almost the same, choose one. Answer every question.

4. *Be prepared for an open book test.* Put tabs on the important pages of your text so that you can retrieve them easily. Number your notes and write a short table of contents. Try devising a one page sheet of formulas, facts, mnemonics, hints, and important names and dates. This way you will not have to hunt for them throughout your book or notes, wasting precious time. Prepare thoroughly. These tests are usually the most difficult!

5. *Stop, think, and write good essay questions.* Good essay responses start with reading the question completely and then responding directly to what has been asked. Many times, students compose answers which have nothing to do with the question posed. It is critical to read for meaning. Following this, brainstorm components to your response, jotting them down on the side margin or on a separate piece of paper.

The ideas from this brainstorm will help generate a short outline. You can use this outline to work your way through the question. Although it seems as though you are using too much time to brainstorm and outline, you will save time in the actual writing and your response will be much more organized and cogent.

6. *Review your responses and answer every question.* Be sure to review all of your answers. Generally, the first answer you chose will be the correct one. Change an answer only if you feel very strongly that you made a mistake. Also, make sure that every question is completed. Even if you are unsure of an answer, put something down. You may get lucky!

7. *Use a positive mental attitude.* All of us face testing anxiety. We can dispel much of this anxiety, however, by telling ourselves positive statements. Say, "I'm doing just fine because I studied for the test," or "I'll take this test carefully so I won't miss anything." By telling ourselves that we know we can succeed, our confidence is invariably raised, as are our grades.

8. *Analyze your test performance.* When you get your test back, note what you missed and why you missed it. Study your errors so you will not repeat that type of mistake. Use your test experience to give your instructor positive feedback, but do not argue incessantly. If you are really disturbed, make an appointment to discuss your concerns and solutions individually.

Effective study skills are a unique blend of organizing your time and work, interacting efficiently with the material, and taking tests in a prepared and "street smart" manner. The combination of these strategies will cut your studying time considerably and also allow you to remember more of the material you need to learn.

Remember, the discipline and skills you bring to your studying are all within your control. No one but you can force you to study too much or too little. Use your time and energies wisely and studying will become a manageable and even enjoyable task.

Again, the strong role that positive attributions play in your studying are important. It is true that people who believe in themselves often succeed. Visualize your accomplishments, tell yourself you can do it, work hard, and you will find success is real and attainable.

1

THE CONTEXT OF SPECIAL EDUCATION

On July 13, 1990, the Congress voted to accept a House-Senate report on the Americans with Disabilities Act, and send it on to the former President George H. Bush for his signature. This bill was written to bar discrimination against people with disabilities. Senator Tom Harkin from Iowa spoke to support this act and said that he was addressing his comments to his deaf brother:

> Today, Congress opens the doors to all Americans with disabilities," Mr. Harkin said, using sign language as well as words. "Today, we say no to ignorance, no to fear, no to prejudice. (Holmes, 1990, p. 7)

I. IMPORTANT POINTS TO REMEMBER

 ➢ Special education has become controversial.

 ➢ Having a disability does not always mean a handicap.

 ➢ Special education is individualized education that matches each child's specific needs with educational services.

 ➢ All children with disabilities have a right to a free appropriate education delivered in the least restrictive environment.

 ➢ Many different professionals from a wide variety of disciplines work with children who have disabilities.

 ➢ The rights of children with disabilities are articulated and defined in two different ways: legislation and litigation.

II. TIMELINE
Review the timeline presented below. Knowing something about the history of special education might help you understand some of the issues related to students with disabilities.

1799   Victor, the Wild Boy of Aveyron, is discovered in the woods of France, and is brought to Dr. Jean-Marc-Gaspard Itard who begins to work with the boy.

1817   Thomas Hopkins Gallaudet begins the American Asylum for the Education of the Deaf and Dumb.

1825   The House of Refuge, the first institution for juvenile delinquents, is founded in New York.

1832   Samuel Gridley Howe starts the New England Asylum for the Blind.

1846   Edouard Seguin writes the first special education treatise that discusses the needs of children with disabilities.

1848   Samuel Gridley Howe begins the Massachusetts School for Idiotic and Feeble-minded Children.

1876   Seguin starts the first professional organization, The Association of Medical Officers of American Institutions for Idiots and Feebleminded Persons (later called the American Association on Mental Deficiency and now called American Association on Mental Retardation), which is comprised of persons concerned about people with mental retardation in America.

1878   Two special education day classes open in the Cleveland Public Schools.

1884   The first U.S. hospital devoted to children with physical disabilities, Home of the Merciful Savor, is opened in Philadelphia.

1897   The National Education Association (NEA) begins a division for professionals interested in children with special needs — then disbanded in 1918.

1898   Elizabeth Farrell begins "ungraded" classes in New York City.

1905   Most states in America have at least one residential institution where children and adults with disabilities live.

1905   Special education teacher preparation is begun through summer classes offered at the New Jersey Training School for Feebleminded Boys and Girls.

1912   Maria Montessori publishes her methods for working with children with special needs.

1922   Elizabeth Farrell begins the Council for Exceptional Children.

1935   The American Speech and Hearing Association (ASHA) is formed.

1949   The United Cerebral Palsy (UCP) organization begins.

1950   The Association for Retarded Children (now called the Arc).

1959   Bank-Mikkelson suggests the concept of normalization.

1961   The National Society for Autistic Children is formed.

1963   The Association for Children with Learning Disabilities (now called Learning Disabilities Association of America), an organization for professionals concerned about the educational needs of students with learning disabilities, begins.

1968   Epilepsy Foundation of American is founded.

1969   Bengt Nirge of Sweden coins the term, "normalization."

1972   Wolf Wolfensberger brings the normalization movement to the U.S.

1973   Section 504 of the Rehabilitation Act, which prohibits discrimination and protects the rights of persons with disabilities, is enacted.

1975   The Education for all Handicapped Children Act (EHA), PL 94-142 (now called the Individuals with Disabilities Education Act - IDEA), becomes law.

1986   PL 99-457 reauthorizes EHA, mandates services for preschoolers with disabilities, and requires that Individualized Family Service Plans be developed for each child receiving services.

1988   Fair Housing Act Amendments prohibits discrimination in the sale or rental of housing.

1990   The Americans with Disabilities Act (ADA) — which prohibits discrimination in employment, transportation, public accommodations, and telecommunications — is passed.

1990   PL 101-476, the Education of the Handicapped Act (EHA) Amendments of 1990, changes the name of the law to Individuals with Disabilities Education Act (IDEA) and strengthens concepts relating to the transition of adolescents from school to adult life.

1997   IDEA '97 is passed, making major changes in ways students with disabilities are disciplined and receive educational services.

2001   PL 107-110, No Child Left Behind Act of 2001: (ESEA), requires that 95 percent of all schoolchildren be full participants in state and district testing. It also includes as a goal that within 12 years *all* students demonstrate proficiency in reading and mathematics.

III. MAIN IDEAS AND DETAILS

Organize your notes efficiently by listing the *Main Ideas* in one column and relating at least two *Details* to each main idea. The table below was designed to help you organize your thoughts as you study this chapter in your textbook. To assist you, we provided either the *Main Ideas* or parts of the *Details*. Extra room has been provided to add additional topics for you to remember as you study.

Main Ideas	Details
1. Why concepts of disabilities differ	1. Attitudes 2. 3. 4. 5. Culture
2. Individuals associated with the beginnings of special education	1. 2.
3.	1. National Special Education Law passed in 1975
4.	1. Free appropriate public education (FAPE) 2. Least restrictive environment

Main Ideas	Details
5. Advocacy	1. 2. 3.
6. Federal laws that protect the civil rights of children and adults with disabilities	1. 2. 3. 4. 5.
8.	1. Number of cases 2. 12% of schoolchildren
9.	1. 2. 3.
10.	1. 2. 3.

IV. DEFINE THESE TERMS
Define these important terms listed below. Remember, if you get stuck, you may use the glossary in the back of your textbook.

Americans with Disabilities Act

excess cost

Individuals with Disabilities Education Act

litigation

normalization

prevalence

disabilities-studies

mainstreaming

related services

special education

V. ALPHABET SOUP
There are a number of abbreviations used in special education. Identify the following that relate to special education and were discussed in Chapter 1.

AAMR

ADA

ADHD

AOTA

APTA

ASHA

FAPE

IDEA

IEP

LRE

NASW

The Arc

UCP

VI. STUDY ORGANIZERS

1. Many examples from history show that people with disabilities have experienced both humane and cruel treatment. In the boxes below provide examples of each.

Humane Treatment	Cruel Treatment

2. The 13 *federal* categories of special education listed in this text are: (Hint: Alan Drives His Messy Old Silver Van Down Endless Miles on Squishy Tires.)

1.   8.

2.   9.

3.   10.

4.   11.

5.   12.

6.   13.

7.

3. The Name Game:
Briefly identify the important people you should know who were discussed in Chapter 1.

Person	Time Period	Significant Accomplishments
Edouard Seguin		
Elizabeth Farrell		
Thomas Hopkins Gallaudet		
Samuel Gridley Howe		
Jean-Marc-Gaspard Itard		
Maria Montessori		
Paul Marchant		
Victor		

4. Summarize Congress's reasons for a national special education law.

1.	6.
2.	7.
3.	8.
4.	9.
5.	

5. Many problems are associated with special education. List and resolve them below.

Problem	Solution
1.	
2.	
3.	
4.	
5.	
6.	
7.	

6. The courts and the legislature have established rules and regulations about children with disabilities. In Chapter 1, some of those were discussed. Complete the next charts, which will help you learn about these important rulings.

Important Legislation		
Law	Summary	Importance/Finding
Section 504 of the Rehabilitation Act of 1973 (1973)		
Education for all Handicapped Children Act (also called PL 94-142 and EHA) (1975)		
Americans with Disabilities Act (ADA) (1990)		
IDEA '97 (PL 105-17) (1997)		
No Child Left Behind Act of 2001: (ESEA)		

Important Court Cases		
Case	Summary	Importance/Finding
Brown v. Board of Education (1954)		
Pennsylvania Association for Retarded Children (PARC) v. Commonwealth of Pennsylvania (1972)		
Mills v. Board of Education of the District of Columbia (1972)		

VII. WEB ACTIVITIES

 Everyday, more and more information is posted on the internet. This access to information allows for easier and in-depth study on issues and topics. Learning how to negotiate the internet develops a valuable skill which will assist you as you study and work with students with disabilities and their families. The weblinks for these activities, along with many other resources, can be found at the companion website for the text: www.ablongman.com/smith5e.

1. Use the internet to search for the *Annual Report to Congress on the Implementation of IDEA.* Compare the percentage of children in your state receiving special education with other states. Why do you think the percentages vary? What factors might influence prevalence? In what types of classrooms (general, resource, separate, residential, and so on) do they receive their services? Are diverse students disproportionately represented in special education? Here's a web site to get you started: http://www.ideadata.org/

2. What careers are available to those interested in working with students with disabilities and their families? What do these career paths involve? What training is required? Where might you go to school to be prepared for some of these jobs? Try this web site as you begin your search: http://www.special-ed-careers.org/

VIII. FOCUS QUESTIONS
After studying the information presented in the textbook chapter and doing the exercises found in this study guide chapter, you should be able to answer the advance organizer questions listed at the beginning of the textbook chapter. Answer these questions to see if you need to review the material in this workbook and textbook again.

1. What does it mean to have a disability?

2. Where did special education come from, and why did it develop?

3. Why did the federal government and the public call for national intervention?

4. What are some defining features of special education?

5. Why is special education controversial?

6. What are some solutions to problems faced by students with disabilities and the educators charged with meeting their needs?

IX. THINKING ABOUT DILEMMAS TO SOLVE

Consider the following issues. Think broadly about how the dilemmas listed below might be solved in this new century. Remember, no "correct" answers or proven solutions to these problems have been agreed upon (or even tested). Regardless, they are important to students with disabilities and their families.

1. Is having a disability necessarily a handicap? What is a disability and what should society's response to such differences be?

2. Give two examples each of ways that the media portray people with disabilities in a positive and negative light.

3. Do the courts need to continue being involved in issues related to disabilities? At what point might that involvement be unnecessary?

4. How could the perception that special education is problematic be resolved?

5. How do the perspectives of diverse societies and cultures influence the concepts of "disability" and "handicapped"?

X. PUTTING IT ALL TOGETHER
Discussion questions:

a. Does special education segregate children unnecessarily? Is segregation always bad? Why? Why not?

b. Does special education serve too many children? At what point does the number of children served become excessive?

c. Is special education too expensive? Is there any level when it becomes excessive? How should decisions about costs of services be made?

d.   How does the Americans with Disabilities Act help special education?

e. How can the overrepresentation of culturally and linguistically diverse students in programs for students with disabilities be eliminated? Their underrepresentation in gifted education?

XI. PUZZLES: A TIME TO PLAY

Cryptograms are encoded messages; each letter of the alphabet actually represents a different letter (i.e., 'V' represents the letter 'S', 'K' represents the letter 'E', etc. The cryptogram below relates to information found in Chapter 1.

_____ _____ __ _____ _____
VUKWJCN KATWCYJES JV JSAJMJATCNJQKA KATWCYJES

____ _____ ____ _____ _____ _____ ____
YLCY FCYWLKV KCWL WLJNA'V VUKWJGJW SKKAV ZJYL

_____ _____
KATWCYJESCN VKIMJWKV

29

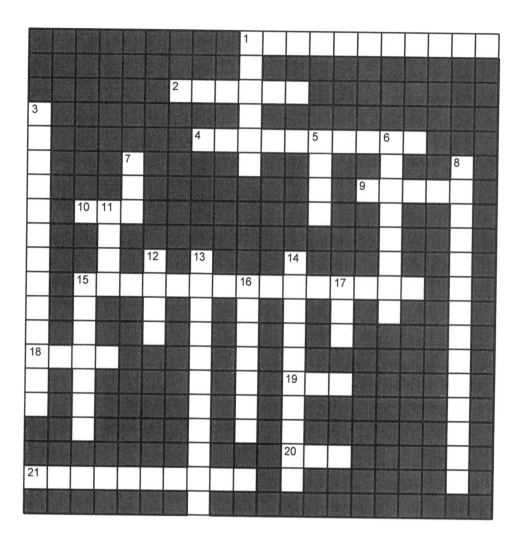

Across
1 Programs by classification
2 Edouard _____
4 A lawsuit or legal proceeding
9 The father of special education
10 Education for All Handicapped Children Act
15 Additional special education services
18 New name given to the EHA
19 Must be balanced with 7 down
20 Council for Exceptional Children (abbr.)
21 Additional expenses for special education

Down
1 Where 4 across occurs
3 Ordinary patterns of life made available
5 American Association on Mental Retardation (abbr.)
6 Results
7 Americans with Disabilities Act (abbr.)
8 Seeking out and designating children who need special education services
11 Founded the New England Asylum for the Blind
12 A principle of IDEA
13 Laws
14 Total number of cases
15 Founder of the World Institute on Disability
16 _____ education
17 Guarantee for individualized services

XII. MAKING CONNECTIONS

Listed below is the website address for The Center of Universal Design. Review this website and then design a three bedroom/two bath home using universal design.

The Center for Universal Design
College of Design
North Carolina State University
50 Pullen Road, Brooks Hall, Room 104
Campus Box 8613
Raleigh, NC. 27695-8613
toll-free : 800.647.6777
ph. 919.515.3082
fax. 919.515.7330
E-mail: cud@ncsu.edu
http://www.design.ncsu.edu/cud/index.html

2

INDIVIDUALIZED SPECIAL EDUCATION PROGRAMS: PLANNING AND DELIVERING SERVICES

George Covington, former Special Assistant to the Vice President of the United States for Disability Policy, helps us put disability into perspective:

> Some of us with disabilities are charming, witty, and highly intelligent; some of us are not. The disability didn't determine which of us would be sexy and which of us would be sexist. A disability gives us a different perspective, not a different personality. (Smith & Plimpton, 1993, p. 29)

I. IMPORTANT POINTS TO REMEMBER

➢ All children with disabilities, ages birth to 21, are entitled to a free appropriate education in the least restrictive environment possible.

➢ Special education is individualized.

➢ Infants, toddlers, and preschoolers with disabilities between the ages of birth and two must have an Individualized Family Service Plan (IFSP).

➢ School age children (3 and older) and youth with disabilities must have an Individualized Educational Program (IEP) developed for them.

➢ Some youth with disabilities, beginning at age 14, have a transition component in their IEP to assist in the transition from school to work and to adult service agencies.

➢ All individualized plans or programs must be evaluated at least annually.

➢ Variations exist in the special education placements used in different states.

II. TIMELINE

Review the timeline presented below. Knowing something about the laws of special education might help you understand some of the issues related to students with disabilities.

1975   The Education for All Handicapped Children Act (EHA and now called Individuals with Disabilities Education Act or IDEA), also known as PL 94-142, becomes law and guarantees students with disabilities a free appropriate public education in the least restrictive environment possible.

1986   PL 94-457 is signed into law; these amendments to the law provide incentives and mandates for states to provide an education to infants, toddlers, and preschoolers ages birth to five.

1990   PL 101-476, the Amendments to EHA of 1990, changes the name of these laws to the Individuals with Disabilities Education Act (IDEA) and strengthens the requirements for youth with disabilities to have transition plans incorporated into their Individualized Education Plans (IEPs).

1997   PL 105-17, IDEA '97, changes the way disruptive students with disabilities are treated, stressed access to the general education curriculum, and their participation in high stakes testing.

2001   "No Child Left Behind Act of 2001" requires annual testing of all children in reading and math.

III. MAIN IDEAS AND DETAILS

Organize your notes efficiently by listing the *Main Ideas* in one column and relating at least two *Details* to each main idea. The table below was designed to help you organize your thoughts as you study this chapter in your textbook. To assist you, we provided either the *Main Ideas* or parts of the *Details*. Extra room has been provided to add additional topics for you to remember as you study.

Main Ideas	Details
1.	1. Pull-in Programming 2. Co-teaching 3. 4. Itinerant or consultative 5. 6. 7. 8.
2. Special Education and Related Service Professionals	1. 2.
3. Participation in the General Education Curriculum	1. 2. Statewide or Districtwide

Main Ideas	Details
4. Critical features of special education programs	1. FAPE 2. 3. 4. Appropriate evaluations 5. 6.
5. Purposes of evaluation	1. 2. Guide Instruction 3.
6. Individualized Education Plans	1. 2. IEP 3.
7.	1. 2.

IV. DEFINE THESE TERMS

Define these important terms listed below. Remember, if you get stuck, you may use the glossary in the back of your textbook.

acuity

accommodations

array of services

assistive technology

audiologist

authentic assessments

cascade of services

center schools

child find

collaboration

continuum of services

due process hearing

evaluation

home or hospital teacher

Individualized Educational Program

Individualized Family Service Plan

judicial hearing

least restrictive environment

occupational therapist

physical therapist

portfolio assessment

pull in programming

school psychologist

school nurses

service manager

service delivery options

speech/language pathologist

V. ALPHABET SOUP

There are a number of abbreviations used in special education. Identify the following that relate to special education, and were discussed in Chapter 2.

CBM

FAPE

IDEA

IEP

IFSP

LRE

SLP

OT

PT

VI. STUDY ORGANIZERS

1. Compare and contrast the different service models below.

	Array of services	Continuum of services	Cascade of services
Definition			
Advantages	1. 2.	1. 2.	1. 2.
Criticisms	1. 2.	1. 2.	1. 2.

2. High stakes testing is an issue facing educators and students with disabilities. Discuss the possible benefits and problems with this process.

Benefits:

Problems:

3. List five principles to consider in the development and implementation of IEPs.

     a.

     b.

     c.

     d.

     e.

4. List six critical features of special education programs, and briefly describe each one.

Feature	Description
1.	
2.	
3.	
4. Appropriate Evaluations	
5.	
6.	

5. List the seven steps in the individualized program plan process. Here is a mnemonic to help you remember: Priscilla **R**uns **E**verywhere, **E**ven **D**own **I**n **A**ustralia.

      a.

      b.

      c.

      d.

      e.

      f.

      g.

SOMETHING TO THINK ABOUT Cost cannot be a factor when determining related service need.

---

6. List the components that should be included in each of the Individualized Education Plans below.

IFSP	IEP	Transition Component
•	•	•
•	•	•
•	•	•
•	•	•
•	•	•
•	•	
•	•	
•	•	
	•	
	•	

VII. WEB ACTIVITIES

 Everyday, more and more information is posted on the internet. This access to information allows for easier and in-depth study on issues and topics. Learning how to negotiate the internet develops a valuable skill which will assist you as you study and work with students with disabilities and their families. The weblinks for these activities, along with many other resources, can be found at the companion website for the text: www.ablongman.com/smith5e.

1. Start to develop a resource file for parents who have a child with a hearing loss. Search the web for information and resources available for your file. Visiting the SHHH web page might be a useful place to begin: http://www.shhh.org.

2. IDEA requires students who are excessively disruptive or who break school conduct codes relating to drugs and weapons have a behavioral intervention plan (BIP) developed for them. Check out the internet to get more information about BIPs and functional assessments than is available in your textbook. Many different sites contain information about BIPs, functional assessments, and students with disabilities who are violent, but a good start might be with the federal Office of Special Education Program's web page and the information they have posted about IDEA: http://www.ed.gov/offices/OSERS/OSEP/

VIII. FOCUS QUESTIONS

After studying the information presented in the textbook chapter and doing the exercises found in this study guide chapter, you should be able to answer the advance organizer questions listed at the beginning of the textbook chapter. Answer these questions to see if you need to review the material in this workbook and textbook again.

1. What are the seven steps to developing an individualized program for each student with disabilities?

2. What roles do the IEP team fill?

3. What factors must be considered when determining the least restrictive environment for individual students?

4. What are the different educational placement options that comprise the continuum for services for special education?

5. What are the different purposes of IDEA's various program plans?

6. How should the array of educational services and supports available to students with disabilities be implemented?

IX. THINKING ABOUT DILEMMAS TO SOLVE

Consider the following issues. Think broadly about how the dilemmas listed below might be solved in this new century. Remember, no "correct" answers or proven solutions to these problems have been agreed upon (or even tested). Regardless, they are important to students with disabilities and their families.

1. When parents and teachers have opposing concepts of LRE for a child, how should it be handled?

2. How might the contentious nature of resolving disputes between schools and families and the process related to due process hearings be reduced?

3. How can IDEA safeguards be ensured and yet not result in complicated or confusing regulations?

4. Is special education and IDEA an unfunded mandate, where the federal government unfairly sets requirements on states and local governments, but does not provide the funding to meet their requirements? Is this a problem that needs a new solution? If so, how should it be solved?

5. How should placement and curricular options be determined for individual students with disabilities?

X. PUTTING IT ALL TOGETHER

Discussion questions:

a. Why do many educators believe that IEPs are a burden? How might that perception be changed?

b. What should be the final result of procedures to follow when students with disabilities are violent, disruptive, or break schools' codes of conduct? Should they be liable to the same consequences as students without disabilities? Should there be any exceptions?

c. How should LRE and FAPE be balanced?

d. What kind and degree of accommodations should students with disabilities receive when they participate in statewide or district-wide assessments? Should all students with disabilities be included?

e. What role should students with disabilities take in the development of their own IEPs? How should differences in perceptions about their goals and educational programs be resolved?

XI. PUZZLES: A TIME TO PLAY

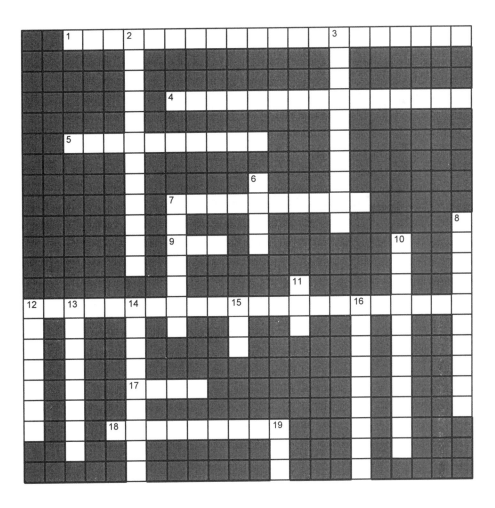

Across

1 _____ assessment: Used to assess a student's problem behaviors
4 Selection of services where step by step movement along the options is not required
5 The second step in the IEP process
7 another word for team teaching
9 This person diagnoses and treats speech and language problems
12 "Array", "cascade", and "continuum" are examples of these
17 Developed for children under age 3
18 A type of assessment that uses student work

Down

2 _____/collaboration teaching
3 Testing
6 Free Appropriate Public Education
7 Linear model of services
8 _____ testing: rewards schools based upon standardized test scores of students
10 Related service professional who diagnoses auditory problems
11 Least Restrictive Environment
12 The age at which the IEP must include a statement of interagency responsibilities and linkages to ensure continuity of services
13 Comes after prereferral and before assessment
14 Graduated range of services where one level leads to the next
15 Blueprint for special education programs
16 A type of authentic assessment
19 A data collection system of evaluation

XII. MAKING CONNECTIONS

The Office of Special Education and Rehabilitation Services has a website titled "A Guide to the Individualized Education Program". Listed below is the address for the website. Review this website and then click on to "Sample IEP form". Use this form to create an IEP for the scenario below.

http://www.ed.gov/offices/OSERS/OSEP/Products/IEP_Guide/

Susie is a first grader in Mrs. Flippin's class at Hillsboro Elementary School. Susie has a profound hearing loss in both ears and wears two hearing aids. She does not know sign language but reads lips.   Susie is doing well with her math and reading but is struggling in spelling, dictation and oral language skills. Susie's parents feel that LRE for her would be full inclusion in the classroom with resource help as needed. Create an IEP that would give Susie the resources that she needs to successfully participate in the general education classroom.

3

MULTICULTURAL AND BILINGUAL SPECIAL EDUCATION

A little black girl yearns for the blue eyes of a little white girl, and the horror at the heart of her yearning is exceeded only by the evil of fulfillment. (Morrison, 1970, p. 158)

I. IMPORTANT POINTS TO REMEMBER

> ➢ Diverse students are overrepresented in special education.

> ➢ In multicultural and bilingual special education, the special education needs of culturally and linguistically diverse students with disabilities are primary.

> ➢ Poverty affects a large number of culturally and linguistically diverse students, and its consequences are often confused with the effects of language and cultural differences.

> ➢ Poverty increases risk for disabilities.

> ➢ The number of multicultural and bilingual students in the U.S. is increasing rapidly

> ➢ Multicultural and bilingual special education is not a disability category, but many of these students do have additional special needs.

> ➢ Discriminatory testing is a risk when identifying culturally and linguistically diverse students with disabilities.

> ➢ The acquisition of conversational skills does not guarantee proficiency in the complex language abilities required for academic learning.

II. TIMELINE

Review the timeline presented below. Knowing something about the history of multicultural and bilingual education might help you understand some of the issues related to culturally and linguistically diverse students with disabilities.

1694 to the early 20th century	Separate schools for German and other immigrants are operating.
Before 1960s	The "melting pot" model of homogenizing people into American 1960s society is popular.
1960s	The "renaissance" of bilingual education is achieved.
1960s	Cultural pluralism begins to replace the "melting pot" model.
1968	Bilingual Education Act (PL 90-247) is signed by President Lyndon Johnson.
1968	"Is Special Education Justifiable?" is written by Lloyd Dunn and published in *Exceptional Children.*
1970	The President's Committee on Mental Retardation publishes the "Six Hour Retarded Child."
1970	*Diana v. State Board of Education* in California focuses on issues of nondiscriminatory testing.
1971	*Larry P. v. Riles* brings to the attention of the courts in California the overrepresentation of African-American students in classes for students with mental retardation and the possibility of discrimination in intelligence testing.
1973	Jane Mercer publishes "Labeling the Mentally Retarded," raises important issues relating to labeling and identification of culturally and linguistically diverse students with disabilities, and proposes solutions to these problems.
1974	The U.S. Supreme Court rules in *Lau v. Nichols* that English-only education provided to students who cannot speak English is not equal access to the educational system.

| 1978 | Mercer and Lewis develop the *System of Multicultural Pluralistic Assessment (SOMPA)*, the first systematic attempt to measure and interpret sociocultural variables when identifying culturally and linguistically diverse students with disabilities. |

| 1980 | In the case of *Parents in Action on Special Education (PASE) v. Hannon,* a federal judge in Illinois rules that standardized tests of intelligence are not discriminatory when used to identify students with disabilities. |

| 1982 | In the case of *Plyler v. Doe,* the Supreme Court decides that all children, including undocumented Mexican nationals, have a right to a free public education. |

| 1983 | Donna Gollnick and Phil Chinn publish the first edition of their classic text about multicultural education. |

| 1994 | California voters pass Proposition 187, prohibiting undocumented immigrants from receiving public benefits, including education. |

| 1998 | California voters passes Proposition 227 which banned bilingual education. |

| 1999 | Twenty-five states have passed "English Only" laws. |

III. MAIN IDEAS AND DETAILS

Main Ideas	Details
1. Multicultural and bilingual special education defined	1. 2. 3. 4. 5.

Main Ideas	Details
2. Identification	1. History of over-identification and discrimination 2. Difficult to diagnose children who have difficulty with English 3. Inadequate assessment instruments and procedures 4.
3. History of the field	1. 2. 3.
4. Prevalence	1. 2. 3.
5.	1. Effects of poverty are confused with effects of diversity 2. 3.

Main Ideas	Details
6. Exceptional culturally and linguistically diverse children	1. 2. 3.
7. Educational interventions	1. 2. 3. 4.
8. Families	1. 2.
9. Technology	1. 2.
10	1. 2.

IV. DEFINE THESE TERMS

Define these important terms listed below. Remember, if you get stuck, you may use the glossary in the back of your textbook.

at risk

basic interpersonal communication
skills (BICS)

bilingual maintenance approach

bilingual transitional approach

code switching

cognitive/academic linguistic
proficiency (CALP)

computerized language translators

cooperative learning

cross-cultural dissonance

cultural pluralism

demographics

dialect

Ebonics

English as a Second Language

English Language Learners

extended family

Limited English Proficiency

melting pot

multiple intelligences

nondiscriminatory testing

overrepresentation

sheltered instruction

total immersion

underrepresentation

V. ALPHABET SOUP
There are a number of abbreviations used in special education. Identify the following that relate to special education and were discussed in Chapter 3.

CYC

ESL

ELL

IQ

LEP

LRE

PCMR

SES

SOMPA

VI. STUDY ORGANIZERS

1. Describe where discrimination can occur in the testing process and explain how it can happen:

Where	Explanation
1.	
2.	
3.	
4.	

2. The Name Game: Briefly identify the important people you should know who were discussed in Chapter 3.

Person	Time Period	Significant Accomplishments
Leonard Baca / Hermes Cervantes		
Phil Chinn / Donna Gollnick		

Lloyd Dunn		
Jane Mercer		

3. The courts have established rules and regulations about culturally and linguistically diverse students with disabilities. In Chapter 3, some of those were discussed. Complete the next chart that will help you learn about these important rulings.

Important Court Cases

Case	Summary
Diana v. State Board of Education (1970)	
Larry P. v. Riles (1971)	
Lau v. Nichols (1974)	
Phyler v. Doe (1982)	

4. This chart describes two unique areas where culturally and linguistically diverse students with disabilities may have problems:

Area	Description
1.	
2.	

5. List accommodations that teachers can make for culturally and linguistically diverse students.

    a.

    b.

    c.

    d.

6. Five basic approaches are used with bilingual students. Name, define, and summarize the advantages and disadvantages of each approach.

Approach	Definition	Advantage/Disadvantage
1.		
2.		
3.		
4.		
5.		

7. List five critical components that make for effective instruction for ELL students.

    a.

    b.

    c.

    d.

    e.

VII. WEB ACTIVITIES

The weblinks for these activities, along with many other resources, can be found at the companion website for the text: www.ablongman.com/smith5e.

1. Cultural diversity can be a great resource to teachers as they make the curriculum and instruction more relevant to every student. However, knowing about all of the different cultures students bring to school is impossible. Fortunately, information that may assist teachers in planning culturally relevant activities is available on many different web sites. Here's a place to start: http://www.tesol.edu

2. Issues surrounding linguistically diverse students seem to constantly be changing, as states and districts modify their policies about bilingual education, instruction of ELL students, and ESL. Identify the most current issues being debated in your state and at the national level as they relate to linguistically diverse students. The National Association of Bilingual Education provides current information about pending legislation, court cases, and discussions among policy makers: http://www.nabe.org

---

SOMETHING TO THINK ABOUT Current trends indicate that by the year 2009, 40% of public school students but only 12% of teachers will be from diverse backgrounds.

VIII. FOCUS QUESTIONS

After studying the information presented in the textbook chapter and doing the exercises found in this study guide chapter, you should be able to answer the advance organizer questions listed at the beginning of the textbook chapter. Answer these questions to see if you need to review the material in this workbook and textbook again.

1. What is meant by multicultural special education, and whom do these programs serve?

2. What is considered overrepresentation in special education and underrepresentation in gifted education?

3. Why are educators so concerned about culturally and linguistically diverse children?

4. In what ways can biases occur in the identification and assessment process?

5. How can school personnel integrate children's home cultures and languages into the educational environment and curriculum?

6. What measures can be taken to reduce overrepresentation of culturally and linguistically diverse students in disability categories and their underrepresentation in gifted education?

IX. THINKING ABOUT DILEMMAS TO SOLVE

Consider the following issues. Think broadly about how the dilemmas listed below might be solved in this new century. Remember, no "correct" answers or proven solutions to these problems have been agreed upon (or even tested). Regardless, they are important to students with disabilities and their families.

1. How can we create opportunities for children from cultural and linguistically diverse backgrounds to have equal chances to succeed?

2. What ways might help students with disabilities and their families become better connected and involved with schools?

3. What strategies and procedures would make general education more responsive to diverse learners?

4. How might issues relating to disproportionate representation of diverse students in special education be resolved?

5. How can special education and gifted programs be improved to become even more effective for diverse learners?

X. PUTTING IT ALL TOGETHER

1. Discussion questions:

   a. Would a reduction of poverty in the population cause a drop in children with disabilities? Why or Why not?

   b. What can be done to reduce the drop out rates of diverse students, particularly Hispanic students?

   c. How does instruction have to change to make education more relevant, meaningful, and interesting to all students?

   d. What steps can be taken to make the curriculum and instruction more multiculturally sensitive?

2. Mini-case Study:

   Mam's Case: Mam was born in Cambodia, and came to America with his five brothers and sisters, mother and father, and his aunt and uncle and their family. When Mam was very young, he and his family lived in a refugee camp while they were waiting to come to America. While there, Mam suffered from malnutrition and contracted several diseases resulting in high fevers and ear infections. By the time Mam was seven, his family had arrived in their new homeland, were settled in a small community, and Mam had begun school. He speaks little English and his language skills in his home language are delayed, but Ms. Peters, Mam's second grade teacher, knows none of these facts.

a. What special accommodations might Ms. Peters make for Mam during his first days at school?

b. What steps might Ms. Peters take to help Mam and his family feel comfortable in the school?

c. What procedures might she put into place to assess Mam's abilities?

d. Once Ms. Peters suspects that Mam might have a disability, what does she do?

e. Finish the story.

XI. PUZZLES: A TIME TO PLAY

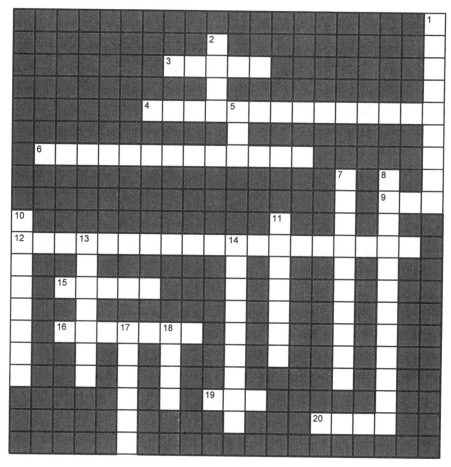

Across

3 _____ v State Board of Education: argued that IQ tests are discriminatory

4 Students taught totally in English

6 Reflecting more than one culture

9 English Language Learners (abbrev.)

12 The lack of presence of a group or groups of individuals in a special education category, as would be predicted by their proportion in the overall school population

15 Test developed by Mercer and Lewis

16 Speech that reflects a region

19 Students whose native language is not English

20 Face-to-face conversational skills (abbrev.)

Down

1 _____ education: Primary instruction in native language until proficient in English

2 Co-author with Cervantes of the Bilingual Special Education Interface

5 _____ v. Nichols: court case on behalf of children with LEP

7 _____ principle: popular theory at the turn of the century

8 The racial and ethnic composition of a country or regional area

10 _____ intelligences

11 _____-only laws

13 A learned and rule-governed, social dialect of nonstandard English, spoken by many African American children

14 type of instruction that restates concepts

17 _____ v. Riles

18 Abstract language abilities required for academics (abbrev.)

XII. MAKING CONNECTIONS

Watch a foreign film without the subtitles. Have a friend watch the same movie with the subtitles. Answer the following questions separately and then compare notes:

1. What was the plot of the movie?

2. List the names of five characters.

3. What were the cultural values in the movie?

4. Did not knowing the language of the movie keep you from enjoying the movie? Why or why not?

SOMETHING TO THINK ABOUT Cultural differences may cause behaviors to be incorrectly interpreted as symptoms of a disability.

4

LEARNING DISABILITIES

P. Buckley Moss, the well-known artist with learning disabilities, describes her school days:

> I was totally unprepared for the discipline of school; and the reading that I knew would be so easy turned out to be a frustration that I could never overcome. Today's educators recognize that many young people suffer a learning disability called dyslexia and, in many, but alas not in all cases, constructive help is given to these children. Not so in my young days when at first I was described as inattentive, then a slow learner, and finally stupid. I tried hard to read. I wanted to be like my sister. I wanted to get it right.... (Moss, 1989, pp. 20-21)

I.   IMPORTANT POINTS TO REMEMBER

➢ Individuals with learning disabilities comprise a heterogeneous group of people.

➢ The unifying difficulty this group of individuals share is an inability to learn at the same rate and manner as their non-disabled peers.

➢ Relatively little is known about the causes of this disability.

➢ Many of these individuals do not approach learning tasks with the same purpose and motivation as their non-disabled peers.

➢ Many of these individuals have difficulties interacting with others in language and social contexts well.

➢ Young children who are late in developing language and develop language in a different sequence tend to be at risk for learning disabilities.

➢ Many individuals with learning disabilities do not reason or solve problems well without direct instruction on these or related skills.

II. TIMELINE

Review the timeline presented below. Knowing something about the history of learning disabilities education might help you understand some of the issues related to students with learning disabilities.

1917	Kurt Goldstein begins work with World War I brain-injured soldiers.
1939	Sam Kirk develops reading drills at the Wayne County Training Center.
1957	New York Association for Brain-injured Children is formed.
1961	Sam Kirk, Jeanne McCarthy, and Winnie Kirk develop the ITPA.
1963	Sam Kirk coins the term "learning disabilities."
1963	Association for Children with Learning Disabilities is formed.
1966	Task forces sponsored by the federal government begin wrestling with definitions for this population of learners.
1968	Division for Learning Disabilities is formed within the Council for Exceptional Children.
1969	PL 91-230, Specific Learning Disabilities Act, is passed by Congress.
1974	The Process/Product Debate engages the field.
1978	The federal government funds five research institutes in learning disabilities.
1978	The National Joint Committee on Learning Disabilities is formed.
1981	The National Joint Committee proposes a new definition of learning disabilities.
1982	The Division for Learning Disabilities becomes an independent professional organization and changes its name to Council for Learning Disabilities.
1982	Council for Exceptional Children forms a new learning disabilities division, the Division for Learning Disabilities.
1997	Attention Deficit Hyperactivity Disorder (ADHD) is called out in IDEA under the health impairments category.

III. MAIN IDEAS AND DETAILS

Main Ideas	Details
1. Learning Disabilities defined	1. 2.
2.	1. 2. Mathematics disability 3.
3. Identification	1. 2. 3. 4.
4. Prevalence	1. 2. Cost 3.

Main Ideas	Details
5. Characteristics	1. 2. 3. 4. 5.
6.	1. 2. 3. Early reading intervention
7. Elementary through high school	1. 2. 3.
7. Social skills characteristics	1. 2. 3. 4.

Main Ideas	Details
8. ADHD	1. 2. 3. 4.
9.	1. letter naming 2. sentence memory 3. quick word decoding 4.
10. Successful collaboration requires	1. 2. 3. 4.
11. Adult outcomes	1. 2.
12.	1. 2. Homework 3.

IV. DEFINE THE TERMS

Define these important terms listed below. Remember, if you get stuck, you may use the glossary in the back of your textbook.

advance organizers

anchored instruction

association

attention deficit hyperactivity disorder (ADHD)

attention deficits

attribute treatment interaction approach

attributions

best practices

central nervous system dysfunction

chunking

classifying

cognitive behavior modification

computer assisted instruction (CAI)

computer-enhanced instruction

curriculum based measurement

direct instruction

discrepancy formulas

discrepancy scores

dyslexia

heterogeneity

hypermedia

hyperactivity

hypertext

impulsive

inactive learners

information processing

lateral dominance

learned helplessness

learning strategies

life skills

low achievers

mathematics/learning disabilities

metacognition

mnemonics

motivation

organizing routines

phonological awareness

problem solving

process/product debate

postsecondary

reading/learning disabilities

resistance to treatment

reversals

scientifically validated interventions

selective attention

self-management techniques

sequencing

social competence

socioeconomic status

standard scores

social competence

unexpected underachievement

word banks

V. ALPHABET SOUP

There are a number of abbreviations used in special education. Identify the following that relate to special education and were discussed in Chapter 4.

ADD

ADHD

CAI

CBM

GED

HOMES

IQ

ITPA

LD

LDA

LDDI

NJCLD

PALS

VI. STUDY ORGANIZERS

1. Many professionals in special education are concerned about the disproportionate number of students labeled as having learning disabilities. Completing the table below should help you better understand the issues, the dilemmas professionals face, and some possible solutions. (Hint: See the section on Prevalence in Chapter 4.)

	Concern	Solution	Implications of Solution
1.			
2.			
3.			

SOMETHING TO THINK ABOUT The label *learning disabilities* does not carry with it the stereotypes of many other special education categories.

2.   Below you will find a partially completed web about ways students with learning disabilities can learn more effectively and efficiently. By completing this web, you should understand various educational approaches and instructional tactics better.

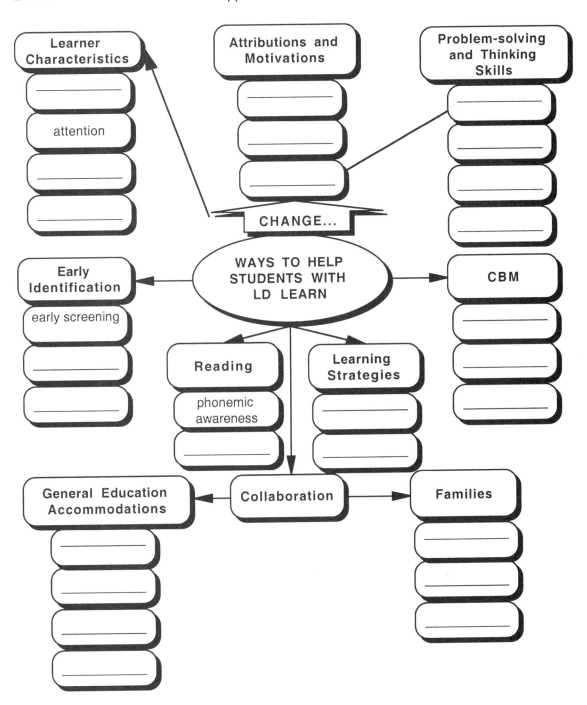

3.   The Name Game

Person	Time Period	Significant Accomplishments
Doug and Lynn Fuchs		
Marianne Frostig		
Kurt Goldstein		
Newell Kephart		
Sam Kirk		
Laura Lehtinen		
Samuel Orton		
Alfred Strauss/ Heinz Werner		

Don Hammill/Steve Larsen		

4. The chapter discussed how students with learning disabilities experience success using various technological applications. Complete the table below by listing the type of technology and the benefits it provides.

Type of Technology	Benefits
1. Hypertext	
2.	
3.	
4.	
5. Word processing	

VII. WEB ACTIVITIES

 Everyday, more and more information is posted on the internet. This access to information allows for easier and in-depth study on issues and topics. Learning how to negotiate the internet develops a valuable skill which will assist you as you study and work with students with disabilities and their families. The weblinks for these activities, along with many other resources, can be found at the companion website for the text: www.ablongman.com/smith5e.

1. Conduct an analysis of the prevalence of students with learning disabilities in your state and across the nation. See if you can identify reasons, from the data, for continual increases in the percentage of students being identified as having this disability. Also, try to determine whether diverse students are overrepresented in this special education category. In addition to your state's department of education home page, remember to review data provided through the *Annual Report to Congress on the Implementation of IDEA*, which is available on the web through: http://www.ideadata.org/

2. You have a college friend who has just been identified as having a learning disability, and you want to help your friend by locating an array of possible supports. Make a list of such supports (at school, in the community, and across the nation), and identify how they might be helpful. You might begin your search with the Learning Disabilities Association of America: http://www.ldanatl.org

VIII. FOCUS QUESTIONS

After studying the information presented in the textbook chapter and doing the exercises found in this study guide chapter, you should be able to answer the advance organizer questions listed at the beginning of the textbook chapter. Answer these questions to see if you need to review the material in this workbook and textbook again.

1. What are the key features of most definitions of learning disabilities?

2. Why is there a call for a new definition, and how might it be different?

3. Why is it correct to consider learning disabilities a lifelong condition?

4. What are some learning characteristics that contribute to these students' poor academic performance?

5. How might the array of services be re-conceptualized for students with learning disabilities?

6. What constitutes an appropriate education for these students, and in what setting should it be provided?

IX. THINKING ABOUT DILEMMAS TO SOLVE

Consider the following issues. Think broadly about how the dilemmas listed below might be solved in this new century. Remember, no "correct" answers or proven solutions to these problems have been agreed upon (or even tested). Regardless, they are important to students with disabilities and their families.

1. Should learning disabilities be discontinued as a special education category and be replaced with a more general "high incidence" special education category combining all mild disabilities?

2. Should the size of this category be limited?

3. Should the operational definition of learning disabilities be made more restrictive or specific?

4. Is it possible to develop instructional practices that are effective for all students with learning disabilities regardless of severity or specific problems? If so, how?

5. How can parents and teachers become better informed about the effectiveness of programs and procedures available?

X. PUTTING IT ALL TOGETHER

1. Discussion Questions:

   a. What are ways to improve the reading abilities of all students?

   b. Discuss some reasons for the high drop out rate of students with learning disabilities.

   c. How might the drop out rate be reduced?

   d. What should the curriculum be for students with learning disabilities?

   e. What supports are needed for these students to succeed in post secondary education?

2. Mini-case studies

   Carlos' story: Carlos, now a third grader, attended a special preschool for English Language Learners beginning when he was three years old. Carlos' family immigrated from Central America when the American government gave them political asylum. When Carlos was an infant, his family experienced considerable hardship due to civil war in their homeland. Carlos' teacher is concerned about him because he is having trouble communicating with others and he is falling behind his classmates academically.

a. Before making a special education referral, what information should Carlos' teacher collect?

b. In the process of collecting data for the pre-referral team, the teacher thinks that she discovered that Carlos is experiencing language delays in both Spanish and English. What should she do next?

c. Does he have a learning disability? If so, what were the indicators? If not, why not? Might he have a different disability?

d. What kinds of special education services should the team consider?

e. Finish the story.

SOMETHING TO THINK ABOUT Before IDEA, most students with ADHD were served in the LD or EBD categories. Now most of these children are identified as belonging in the health impairments category. However, most still receive services alongside their LD or EBD peers.

IX. PUZZLES: A TIME TO PLAY

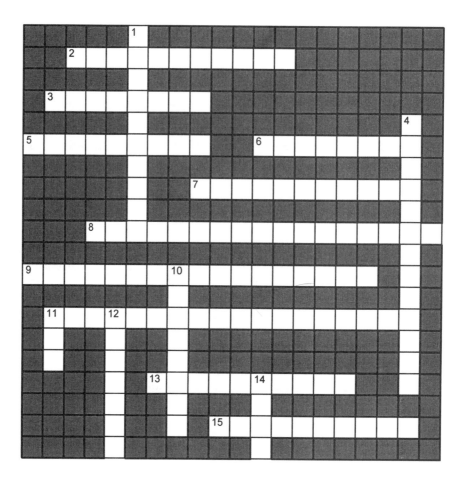

Across

2 inability to sit or concentrate for long periods of time

3 _____-enhanced instruction: software programs which supplement instruction

5 A learning strategy which associates the first letter of items in a list with a word, sentence, or picture

6 A type of learner who does not become involved in learning situations

7 Impaired ability to perform mathematical functions

8 _____ _____ modification: self-talk is an example of this

9 An oral language skill that enables children to understand that words can be represented in print

11 _____ Interaction Approach: Selecting instructional methods that match a student's modality strength

13 Skills used to succeed in personal living environments

15 Methods to increase student success by increasing information collection and organization

Down

1 Categorizing items in order according to various characteristics

4 Understanding one's own learning process

10 Grouping information into smaller pieces to enhance memory

11 A condition which is NOT a disability category (abbrev.)

12 The area in which most students with LD have problems

14 The father of LD

The puzzle below contains a statement concerning one common characteristic of all individuals with learning disabilities. The letters in the columns above the puzzle have been scrambled. You must decide which box below the column each letter fits into. We have helped you with Column 4. Good luck!

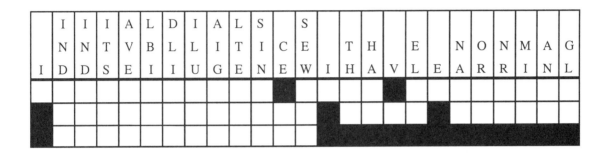

XII. MAKING CONNECTIONS

The IRIS website is an excellent place to obtain course enhancement materials on special education topics. The website also has several modules that are very helpful. Go to http://iris.peabody.vanderbilt.edu/onlinemodules.html and click on to the elementary reading module. Work through the module and answer the questions.

5

SPEECH OR LANGUAGE IMPAIRMENTS

Laureen Summers has cerebral palsy, and explains some of the challenges she faces:

> The greatest problem is the attitude. People don't get enough information, and they make assumptions. People often think I'm mentally retarded because of my speech. Sometimes when I would try to explain, people would nod and go "uh-huh, uh-huh." (Smith & Plimpton, 1993, p. 159)

I.   IMPORTANT POINTS TO REMEMBER

➢ Articulation is the most common speech or language impairment.

➢ Speech impairments are more common among young children.

➢ Four out of five dysfluent children make a spontaneous recovery during childhood and do not become stutterers.

➢ Systematic, well-organized preschool experiences should be available to all children who exhibit speech or language impairments, as well as those who are considered at risk.

➢ Young children with language impairments have a high probability for academic difficulties, and later being reclassified as having learning disabilities.

➢ Language instruction and experiences should be part of all children's educational curricula.

➢ Communicative competence is the overall goal for students with speech and language impairments.

II. TIMELINE

Review the timeline presented below. Knowing something about the history of speech and language education might help you understand some of the issues related to students with speech and language impairments.

1000 BC	Speech and language problems is recognized, but individuals with these impairments were considered fools or buffoons.
1910	First public school speech correction services begin in Chicago.
1913	Speech correction programs begin in the public schools in New York.
1914	Smiley Blanton opens the first speech clinic at the University of Wisconsin.
1919	Wyoming appoints a state director of special education whose partial responsibility is to provide for speech defective children.
1921	University of Wisconsin, the first university training program, graduates the first doctorate in speech impairments, Sara Stinchfield.
1925	Robert West, considered the father of this field, is one of the founders of the American Academy for Speech Correction (later called American Speech-Language-Hearing Association or ASHA).
1938	The Coyne Voice Pitch Indicator shows voice pitch through a visual image.
1940s	The American military provides services for speech and hearing.
1959	Funding for speech and language services in schools is provided in 39 states.
1961	PL 87-276 provides funding to prepare teachers of those with speech and hearing impairments.
1975	A computerized speech synthesizer is developed to help persons with severe motoric and speech impairments make spoken statements.

III. MAIN IDEAS AND DETAILS

Organize your notes efficiently by listing the *Main Ideas* in one column and relating at least two *Details* to each main idea. The table below was designed to help you organize your thoughts as you study this chapter in your textbook. To assist you, we provided either the *Main Ideas* or parts of the *Details*. Extra room has been provided to add additional topics for you to remember as you study.

Main Ideas	Details
1.	1. Speech Impairments 2. Language Impairments
2. Speech impairments	1. 2. 3.
3. Language impairments	1. 2. 3.
4. Prevalence	1. 2.

Main Ideas	Details
5. Causes	Speech Impairments 1. 2. 3. 4. 5. 6. Language Impairments 1. 2. 3. 4.
6. Prevention	1. 2. 3. 4.

Main Ideas	Details
7. Characteristics	Speech Impairments 1. 2. 3. 4. Language Impairments 1. 2. 3. 4. 5. 6.
8. Teachers' instructional supports	1. 2.

Main Ideas	Details
9. Content enhancement strategies	1. 2. 3. 4.
10. Collaboration for inclusion	1. 2. 3.
11. Transition through adulthood	1. 2. 3.
12. Families	1. 2.
13. Technology	1. 2.

Main Ideas	Details
14.	1.
	2.

IV. DEFINE THESE TERMS

Define these important terms listed below. Remember, if you get stuck, you may use the glossary in the back of your textbook.

alternative and augmentative communication

aphasia

articulation problems

barrier games

cleft palate

collaborative consultation

communication

communication competence

communication signals

communication symbols

content

content enhancement strategies

dysfluencies

environmental restructuring

figurative language

fluency problems

follow-up study

form

instructional supports

language

language delay

language different

language impairment

loudness

morphology

obturator

otitis media

phonology

pitch

pragmatics

respiratory system

resonating system

semantics

sign language

speech

speech impairments

speech mechanisms

speech synthesizers

stuttering

syntax

use

vibrating system

voice problems

written symbols

V. ALPHABET SOUP

There are a number of abbreviations used in special education. Identify the following that relate to special education and were discussed in Chapter 5.

AAC

ASHA

CCC

CLAS

PLDK

PPC

SLP

VI. STUDY ORGANIZERS

1. To help you better understand the process of communication, fill in the diagram below.

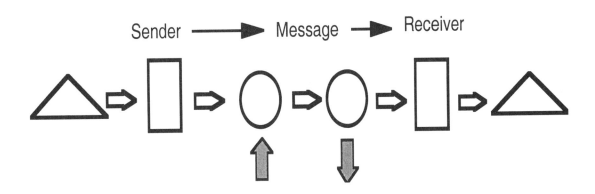

2. To understand how speech is produced, it is helpful to be able to trace the actions that must occur for an individual to speak. Use the space below to sketch a picture of the upper part of the human body (figure 5.2 in your text). Then label the different mechanisms, systems, and organs used to produce speech. Also, talk to yourself as you describe how the entire process occurs.

SOMETHING TO THINK ABOUT There is a strong correlation between language impairments and learning disabilities.

3. The Name Game

Person	Time Period	Significant Accomplishments
Smiley Blanton		
Robert West		
Lee Travis		
Wendell Johnson		

4. List four general methods teachers can utilize help students develop communication skills and give an example of each.

Method	Example
1.	
2.	
3.	
4.	

VII. WEB ACTIVITIES

The weblinks for these activities, along with many other resources, can be found at the companion website for the text: www.ablongman.com/smith5e.

1. You need to prepare a report to a local school district board about the various roles that speech/language pathologists are filling today. To get the background information you need to include in this report you should search out as much information as possible. You might start your internet search by checking out the web site for the American Speech and Hearing Association: www.asha.org

2. Search the internet to identify companies that sell alternative and augmentative communication (ACC) devices. Develop a plan for a student you describe as having a specific disability. You might find that information from INTELLITOOLS is a good starting point: www.intellitools.com

VIII. FOCUS QUESTIONS

After studying the information presented in the textbook chapter and doing the exercises found in this study guide chapter, you should be able to answer the advance organizer questions listed at the beginning of the textbook chapter. Answer these questions to see if you need to review the material in this workbook and textbook again.

1. What comprises speech impairments and language impairments?

2. What is the prevalence of this disability?

3. How do language delays, language differences, and language impairments differ?

4. How can teachers enhance language development and help to remediate a language impairment?

5. What is alternative and augmentative communication, and what are its benefits to this population of learners?

6. How might the general and special education curricula be modified to better develop language and literacy abilities of students? How can speech/language pathologists help?

IX. THINKING ABOUT DILEMMAS TO SOLVE

Consider the following issues. Think broadly about how the dilemmas listed below might be solved in this new century. Remember, no "correct" answers or proven solutions to these problems have been agreed upon (or even tested). Regardless, they are important to students with disabilities and their families.

1. What type of training do teachers need in the area of language?

2. What type of support services should SLPs provide to assist with students' literacy development?

3. How can the delivery systems be changed so all students can receive a language-rich education?

4. Should the general education curriculum be modified to specifically address language development?

5. Should there be more instructional materials available that will specifically address language development?

X. PUTTING IT ALL TOGETHER

1. Discussion Questions:

   a. What kind of strategies can parents use at home to improve language skills?

   b. What support services do students and teachers need from SLPs?

c. Why are so many more young children identified as having language impairments and so many more older students classified as having learning disabilities? Is there a problem with this situation?

d. How can teachers assist ELLs in their complete mastery of English?

e. Describe the different kinds of ACC that would be useful in the classroom for a student with language or speech impairment.

2. Mini-case Study:

The purpose of mini-case studies presented in this study guide is to help you extend your knowledge to application situations. There is no single answer to any of the mini-cases, but you should make notes to yourself about how you would support and justify your answer.

Jessica's Case: Jessica was identified as having a language delay before she was three years old. She was first labeled as "at risk" when she was two and half years old, and from that time on she attended early intervention programs. Between the ages of three and five, Jessica attended a specialized preschool program for children with language impairments. Her progress was excellent, and from the first grade to the present Jessica has attended general education classes and received some supportive help from an SLP. Jessica is now in fourth grade, and is having great difficulty in all of her academic subjects. It seems she can no longer keep up with her classmates, whom she has attended school with since first grade. Jessica is a very social child, and she has many friends among her classmates and does not want to go to another school or another class without her friends.

a. What kinds of educational placements should the special services committee consider for Jessica? What factors must they consider when making placement decisions?

b. What kinds of related services should Jessica receive?

c. How much should Jessica participate in the decision about her educational program?

d. Finish Jessica's story.

XI. PUZZLES: A TIME TO PLAY

Solve the cryptogram below. (Hint: The topic is *professional teamwork*.)

_____ _____ _____ ___ _____ _____
_____.
JTLLSKTISWCZH   JTBNYLWSWCTB   CN   S   NDSIHA
IHNUTBNCKCLCWX

____ _____ _____ !
CW   IHVYCIHN   WHSRFTIE

	J								L																
A	B	C	D	E	F	G	H	I	J	K	L	M	N	O	P	Q	R	S	T	U	V	W	X	Y	Z

SOMETHING TO THINK ABOUT It is important to provide services to the child as soon as a speech or language impairment is recognized.

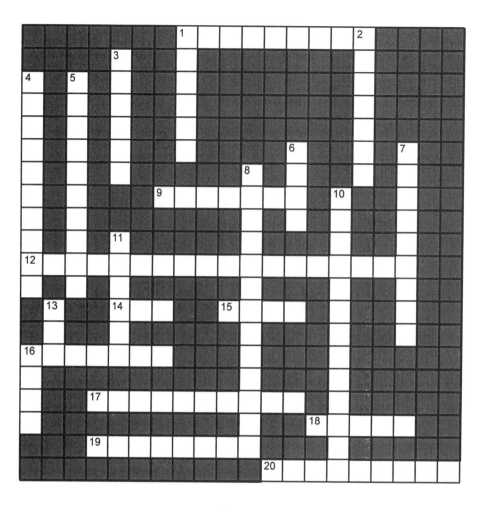

Across

1 The system that governs content, intent and meaning.

9 Used to relay communication messages

12 _____ strategies: Visual organizers of semantic information used in content instruction to teach concepts and vocabulary

14 Alternative and augmentative communication (abbrev.)

15 The rule system of language

16 Loss or impairment of language ability due to brain injury

17 _____ system: where speech sounds are formed

18 High or low quality of voice

19 Formal method of communication

20 Language rules of speech sounds to form words and sentences

Down

1 Determines where a word is placed in a sentence.

2 Messages that announce events, people, actions, or emotions

3 _____ media: Middle ear infection

4 Language in a particular context

5 Lack of fluency characterized by hesitations or repetitions

6 The father of this field.

7 _____ system: larynx and vocal cords, produces sounds and pitch

8 _____ consultation: Professionals working together to develop and implement students' educational programs

10 The transfer of knowledge, ideas, opinions, and feelings.

11 Development of skills that are slower than normal

13 A professional who works with individuals with speech or language impairments (abbrev.)

16 Professional organization for those who work with children with speech or language impairments

The puzzle below contains a statement regarding a speech or language impairment. The letters in the columns above the puzzle have been scrambled. You must decide which box below the column each letter fits into. We have helped you with Column 4. Good luck!

XII. MAKING CONNECTIONS

Spend two hours of observation with a speech pathologist who works at a hospital. Answer the following questions:

1. Of the clients that the speech pathologist worked with, what was the most common cause of language/speech disorders among these clients?

2. Who are the most difficult clients to rehabilitate and why?

3. Who are the most successful clients to rehabilitate and why?

4. Why did the speech pathologist you observe choose this field for a career?

6

MENTAL RETARDATION

On the occasion of Coach Gene Stallings retirement from University of Alabama, his son Johnny, a man with Down syndrome, was honored by the Paul Bryant Museum staff. Coach Stallings recalls that evening:

> As the night was coming to an end I watched Johnny saying his final farewells. Amid photographs of football greats and showcases of football paraphernalia, I noticed a plaque to his right with a famous quote from Coach Bryant that read: "If you believe in yourself and have dedication and pride and never quit you'll be a winner. The price of victory is high but so are the rewards." In thirty-four short years Johnny had gone from an object of pity, someone to be locked up in an institution, to a man who was not only loved but valued by countless people. It was a dream night and it was all Johnny's. (Stallings & Cook, 1997, p. 213)

I. IMPORTANT POINTS TO REMEMBER

➢ Mental retardation refers to significant limitations in cognitive functioning.

➢ A low IQ score and limitations in adaptive behavior are present.

➢ Mental retardation occurs before age 18.

➢ Early identification and early intervention are critical.

➢ More than 50% of all cases of mental retardation are preventable.

➢ Functional skills are those required by students for everyday life.

➢ Technology can enhance students' skills and give them more control over their environment.

II. TIMELINE

Review the timeline presented below. Knowing something about the history of mental retardation might help you understand some of the issues related to students with mental retardation.

1799   Jean-Marc-Gaspard Itard, a French physician, begins working with Victor, the wild boy of Aveyron.

1848   Samuel Gridley Howe creates the first American institution for people with mental retardation, later known as the Walter E. Fernald State School.

1876   The American Association on Mental Retardation (AAMR) is begun.

1877   Richard Dugdale puts forth the story about the Jukes family.

1896   The first American special class for students with mental retardation is opened in Providence, Rhode Island.

1912   Henry Goddard puts forth the story of the Kallikak family.

1917   All but four states have institutions for people with mental retardation.

1921   The first manual of definitions of mental retardation is published by AAMR.

1954   The Association for Retarded Citizens (The Arc) is founded by a group of concerned parents.

1957   Robert Guthrie develops infant screening proven effective in preventing PKU.

1959   Dr. Rick Heber, Chair of the AAMR Terminology and Classification Committee, publishes a groundbreaking definition of mental retardation in which intellectual ability and adaptive behavior are differentiated.

1960s   A new philosophy is stimulated by Benjt Nirje in Sweden called the normalization movement.

1960s   Jim Lent, of the Mimosa Project at Parsons, Kansas, demonstrates the effectiveness of token economies and behavioral principles with students with disabilities.

1961   President Kennedy calls for a national agenda on mental retardation.

1970s   The People First self-advocacy is established to help people with MR learn about and gain access to their rights as US citizens.

1970   The President's Committee on Mental Retardation publishes "The Six Hour Retarded Child."

1972   Wolf Wolfensberger uses the principle of normalization to call for closure of all US institutions and begins a movement towards deinstitionalization of individuals with MR.

1973   Jane Mercer publishes *Labeling the Mentally Retarded,* and raises important issues and solutions relating to labeling and identification of culturally and linguistically diverse students with disabilities.

1983   AAMR publishes a new definition of mental retardation.

1985   The U.S. Supreme Court rules in *City of Cleburne, Texas v. Cleburne Living Centers* that prejudices and stereotypes cannot justify discrimination against people with mental retardation.

1989   Anthony K. Shriver establishes Best Buddies to link college students with mental retardation for support.

1989   Christopher Burke, a young man with Down syndrome, begins acting in a regular television series, "Life Goes On."

1991   The people of New Hampshire resolve to close their remaining institution for individuals with mental retardation and become the first state to pledge that all individuals with mental retardation will live community-integrated lives.

1992   AAMR promulgates a new definition of mental retardation.

2002   A new definition of mental retardation adopted by AAMR.

SOMETHING TO THINK ABOUT Students with mental retardation are less likely to be included in general education classes than students with other types of disabilities.

III. MAIN IDEAS AND DETAILS

Main Ideas	Details
1. Mental retardation defined	1. 2. 3. 4. 5.
2.	1. Intellectual functioning 2. 3. Systems of support
3. History of the field	1. 2. 3. 4. 5.
4.	1. 2. Mental age 3.

Main Ideas	Details
5. Prevalence	1. 2.
6.	1. Prenatal 2. 3. Postnatal
7. Prevention	1. 2. 3. 4.
8.	1. 2. Adaptive behavior 3.
9. Early childhood education	1. 2.

Main Ideas	Details
10.	1. Functional curriculum 2. Community based instruction 3. 4.
11. Collaboration for inclusion	1. 2.
12. Transition through adulthood	1. 2. 3.
13. Families	1. 2. 3.
14. Technology	1. 2.
15.	1. 2.

IV. DEFINE THE TERMS

Define these important terms listed below. Remember, if you get stuck, you may use the glossary in the back of your textbook.

adaptive behavior

adaptive skill areas

anoxia

asphyxia

augmentative communication systems

Best Buddies

chaining

communication board

community based instruction

deinstitutionalization

dignity of risk

Down syndrome

e-buddies

epicanthic fold

eugenics

fetal alcohol syndrome

functional academics

Fragile X syndrome

generic supports

HIV infection

intellectual functioning

job coach

job developer

life skills

mental age

mental retardation

Mimosa Cottage Project

natural supports

nonpaid supports

normalization movement

normal curve

paradigm shift

perinatal

phenylketonuria

postnatal

prenatal

quality of life

self-advocacy movement

self determination

shunt

specialized supports

stereotypic behaviors

supported employment

systems of supports

task analysis

theoretical construct

time delay

time of onset

toxin

trauma

V.   ALPHABET SOUP

There are a number of abbreviations used in special education. Identify the following that relate to special education and were discussed in Chapter 6.

AAMR

AIDS

The Arc

CBI

EMR

FAS

FXS

HIV

MA

PKU

SLP

TMR

VI.   STUDY ORGANIZERS

1. List ten tips that can help teachers working with MR students in generalizing across settings and skills.

1.	6.
2.	7.
3.	8.
4.	9.
5.	10.

2. The Name Game

Person	Time Period	Significant Accomplishments
Richard Dugdale		
Jean-Marc-Gaspard Itard		
Henry Goddard		
Samuel Gridley Howe		
Robert Guthrie		
Charles Klinger		
Jim Lent		
Bengt Nirje		
Bob Perske		
Herb Rieth		
Victor		
Wolf Wolfensberger		

3. There are many causes of mental retardation. AAMR suggests grouping causes by age of onset. Below, identify the three categories of causes of mental retardation, list examples, and provide preventive measures (if available).

Age of Onset	Examples	Prevention
1.	1. 2. 3.	1. 2.
2.	1.	1.
3.	1. 2. 3.	1. 2.

4. Many events can reduce or prevent cases of mental retardation. List seven ways to prevent mental retardation.

1.   6.

2.   7.

3.

4.

5.

5. The learning and physical characteristics of mental retardation should significantly influence how teachers plan and implement educational programs for these students. To help you organize your thoughts on this topic, fill in the chart below.

Characteristic	Ways to Address This Characteristic
1. Communication	
2. Attention	
3. Memory	
4. Generalization	
5. Motivation	

Characteristic	Ways to Address This Characteristic
6. Physical	
7. Stigma of Mental Retardation	

VII. WEB ACTIVITIES

 Everyday, more and more information is posted on the internet. This access to information allows for easier and in-depth study on issues and topics. Learning how to negotiate the internet develops a valuable skill which will assist you as you study and work with students with disabilities and their families. The weblinks for these activities, along with many other resources, can be found at the companion website for the text: www.ablongman.com/smith5e.

1. You are an advocate for individuals with mental retardation and need to develop positions about supports needed for appropriate community presence. Finding position statements from national organizations advocating for persons with mental retardation might be a good place to start:

> http://www.aamr.org
> http://www.familyvillage.wisc.edu/lib_frgx.htm

2. You have been asked to search the internet for sites that help people advocate for individuals with mental retardation. The web sites for many national organizations can help you with your assignment. You might find some parent organizations a good place to start: www.thearc.org

VIII. FOCUS QUESTIONS

After studying the information presented in the textbook chapter and doing the exercises found in this study guide chapter, you should be able to answer the advance organizer questions listed at the beginning of the textbook chapter. Answer these questions to see if you need to review the material in this workbook and textbook again.

1. What are the key components of the 2002 AAMR definition of mental retardation?

2. How are levels of severity and outcomes of mental retardation grouped?

3. How are the causes of mental retardation organized, and what are some of the major causes?

4. What are the four sources of supports?

5. What are some examples of the four levels of support, and how do they make a difference in the lives of people with mental retardation?

6. What are two specialized instructional approaches for students with mental retardation?

7. How can educators be more effective when working with families of students with mental retardation?

IX. THINKING ABOUT DILEMMAS TO SOLVE

Consider the following issues. Think broadly about how the dilemmas listed below might be solved in this new century. Remember, no "correct" answers or proven solutions to these problems have been agreed upon (or even tested). Regardless, they are important to students with disabilities and their families.

1. How can the educational needs of students with mental retardation be best met?

2. How are students with mental retardation prepared for life's challenges through improved access to the general education curriculum?

3. How can society ensure that the history of awful treatment of people with mental retardation not be repeated?

4. What is meant when advocates talk about people with mental retardation achieving a high quality of life?

5. What educational outcomes should families expect for their children?

6. What role do parents play in prevention?

X. PUTTING IT ALL TOGETHER

  1. Discussion Questions:

   a. How can educators come to rely less on intelligence tests and present a more positive view of the condition?

   b. How can we ensure that standards for community living and employment arrangements are of high quality and with sufficient supports?

   c. What types of community residential and employment options need to be developed nationally to have a full array of programs available for people with mental retardation?

   d. How can educators help individuals with moderate and severe disabilities develop meaningful friendships with peers?

e. What supports need to be available to individuals with mental retardation to facilitate their community presence?

2. Mini-case Study:

Stephan's case: Stephan is 10 years old and has received special education services since he was a baby. He has FAS and the doctors diagnosed that he was drug-exposed at birth. Stephan faces many challenges, including having difficulties understanding and predicting consequences to behaviors when interacting with peers.

a. List instructional targets for Stephan.

b. Describe what you believe LRE means for Stephan.

c. Which professionals should be included in his IEP team?

d. Finish Stephan's story.

XI. PUZZLES: A TIME TO PLAY

Solve the puzzle below by unscrambling the letters. Remember, some words may wrap to the next line. (Hint: *a problem encountered by individuals with mental retardation*).

E																		
V		T	A	I				I	C			R	A	J		A	I	
R	E	C	T	D	M	A	I	O	F	N		M	E	N	A	D	E	
P	I	A	N	R	D	S	T	I	O	H	I	M	E	Y	U	T	L	C
N	E	O	P	L	E	D	W	S	T	R	P	M	I	N	T	B	I	O

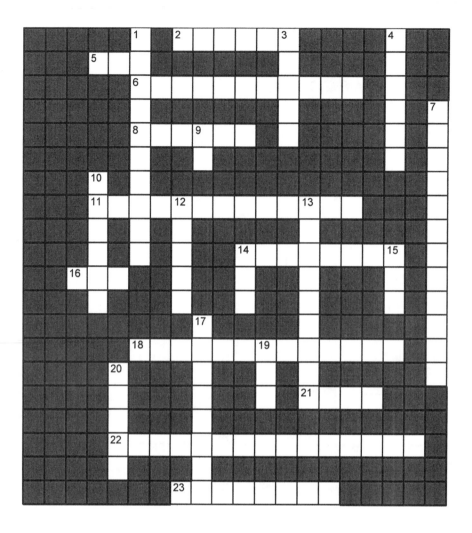

Across

2 Has caused people to say they were in prison rather than admit to having MR
5 A preventable cause of mental retardation (abbr.)
6 Theoretical construct of intelligence
8 Poisonous substances
14 _____ behavior: must be assessed to identify students with MR
16 Condition caused by alcohol abuse (abbr.)
18 Early research site
21 _____ syndrome
22 Ordinary assistance given by friends and neighbors
23 Forward and backward _____

Down

1 _____ academics: utilizes life skills to teach tasks
3 _____ and neglect are causes of MR
4 Itard's student
7 To speak for oneself
9 Is measured on a normal curve
10 Location of 18 across
12 AAMR definition groups causes by time of _____
13 _____ employment
14 Parent association: The _____
15 An old term referring to those with IQs between 50 and 80 (abbr.)
17 Someone who works alongside people with disabilities
19 Instruction in the natural environment (abbr.)
20 A tube which drains fluid from the brain

XII. MAKING CONNECTIONS
Rent and watch the movie "*My Other Sister*". Answer the following questions:

1. What was your overall impression of the movie?

2. List five realistic things as well as five unrealistic things about the movie.

Realistic	Unrealistic
a.	
b.	
c.	
d.	
e.	

3. Do you think such level of independence as portrayed in the movie is possible for someone who has mild mental retardation?

    a. If so, would you recommend the same kind of support used in the movie?

    b. If not, why do you think such level of independence could not be achieved?

SOMETHING TO THINK ABOUT Diverse students are overrepresented in the mental retardation category.

7

GIFTEDNESS AND TALENT DEVELOPMENT

You don't develop world leaders such as Martin Luther King, Golda Meir, and Mahatma Gandhi by having them practice basic skills over and over again or by reiterating mundane concepts that they can undoubtedly learn faster than all of their schoolmates and, in some cases, even many of their teachers. (Renzulli & Reis, 1991, p. 34)

I.   IMPORTANT POINTS TO REMEMBER

➢ The intellectual and artistic abilities of a society should not be neglected, wasted, or squandered.

➢ Intelligence and creativity are not fixed, but rather can be enhanced or inhibited by environmental factors.

➢ Individuals who are gifted and/or talented come from all segments of our society, regardless of gender, ethnicity, or economic background.

➢ Many individuals who are gifted do not receive specialized educational services; services are not consistently delivered across the United States or across time.

➢ Subgroups of gifted learners who are underrepresented in school programs include females, those who are culturally and linguistically diverse, and those with disabilities.

➢ Enrichment approaches allow students to study a subject in more depth and often explore topics not found in traditional curricula.

➢ Acceleration approaches allow students to move through the curriculum at their own pace.

➢ A variety of service delivery options and educational experiences are used with these students.

II. TIMELINE

Review the timeline presented below. Knowing something about the history of giftedness and talent development might help you understand some of the issues related to students with exceptionalities.

1866   A multiple tracking system to allow bright students to advance more rapidly is established in a school in Elizabeth, New Jersey.

1868   The W.T. Harris plan for ability grouping and a flexible system of promotion through elementary grades is developed for gifted students in St. Louis.

1869   Galton's *Heredity Genius* is published.

1898   The Baltimore Plan, adopted in the Chicago Public Schools, provides a three-tiered (dull, normal, and bright) tracking system for students.

1900   The Santa Barbara Concentric Plan tracks students through three homogeneous grouping options per grade.

1900   New York establishes a rapid advancement system for students who are gifted.

1901   Worcester, Massachusetts opens preparatory schools for students who are gifted.

1905   Tests are developed by Binet and Simon (Binet Intelligence Test) for the purpose of identifying students with low intellectual levels.

1910   Lewis Terman begins a longitudinal study of individuals considered geniuses.

1910   The Double Track Plan in Cambridge, Massachusetts implements for students who are gifted.

1911   A survey conducted by the United States Bureau of Education finds 6 percent of cities have special classes for students who are gifted.

1916   Leta Hollingworth at Columbia University teaches the first course about giftedness and wrote the first textbook about gifted children.

1916   Terman's revision of the Stanford-Binet Scale is published.

1920   Cleveland begins special classes for students who are gifted.

1920   Los Angeles begins "enrichment" classes.

1920   Columbia University develops a preparation program for teachers of the gifted.

1922   Terman studies gifted children.

1923   The state of Oregon passes a permissive education act allowing school districts to provide educational services for students who are gifted.

1925   Terman's *The Genetic Study of Genius* is published.

1926   Leta Hollingworth implements enrichment programs for students who are gifted in the New York Public Schools.

1930   The first White House Conference on Child Health and Protection is convened by Herbert Hoover where both children with disabilities and those who are gifted were topics of the conference.

1947   The American Association for Gifted Children is established.

1951   Paul Witty publishes the book, *The Gifted Child*, which causes great interest in gifted education.

1953   The National Association for Gifted Children is established.

1953   Oregon passes permissive legislation for gifted education and reimburses school districts $5,000 for each class.

1957   Sputnik, the Russian space satellite, is launched.

1958   PL 85-864, the National Defense Education Act, funds education of potential leaders.

1970   PL 91-230, the Elementary and Secondary Education Amendments, authorizes funds to be spend on students who are gifted and talented.

1971   The United States Commissioner of Education, Sidney Marland, begins a study of the educational needs of students who are gifted and talented.

1977   June Maker publishes results on subgroup of gifted students: learning disabilities.

1978   PL 95-561, The Gifted and Talented Children's Act passes.

1983   Howard Gardner publishes his book about the theory of multiple intelligences.

1988   The federal definition of Gifted and Talented is re-instituted with a broader orientation toward the concept of gifted education and talent development.

1993   The Jacob Javits Act is passed providing federal funding for research relating to gifted education.

III. MAIN IDEAS AND DETAILS

Main Ideas	Details
1. Giftedness and talent development defined	1. 2. 3. 4. 5.
2. History of the field	1. Egalitarianism 2. 3. Sputnik
3. Prevalence	1. 2. 3.

Main Ideas	Details
4.	1. 2. Heredity 3.
5. Factors that enhance or inhibit creativity	1. 2. 3.
6. Characteristics	1. 2. 3.
7. Subgroups	1. 2. 3. 4.
8.	1. Enrichment 2. Acceleration

Main Ideas	Details
9.	1. 2. 3. pull- out programs 4.
10. Collaboration for inclusion	1. 2.
11. Transition through adulthood	1. 2.
13. Families	1. 2.
14. Technology	1. 2.

IV. DEFINE THE FOLLOWING TERMS:

Define these important terms listed below. Remember, if you get stuck, you may use the glossary in the back of your textbook.

ability grouping

acceleration

advanced placement courses

attributes

categorize

cluster grouping

cooperative learning

creativity

curriculum compacting

differentiated curriculum

egalitarianism

email

eminence

enrichment

Enrichment Triad/Revolving Door Model

gifted

honors sections

independent study

infused

interdisciplinary instruction

internship

longitudinal studies

magnet schools

mentorships

pull-out programs

Sputnik

standard deviation

talent development

telecommunications

twice-exceptional students

worldwide web

V. ALPHABET SOUP
There are a number of abbreviations used in special education. Identify the following that relate to special education and were discussed in Chapter 7.

IQ

SD

WISC III

SOMETHING TO THINK ABOUT A current debate asks: Is it morally right to segregate gifted students or provide them with a unique educational experience?

VI. STUDY ORGANIZERS

1.   Definitions of giftedness and talent development are often used to identify students who are gifted and talented and to guide educators as they develop educational programs. Complete the chart below to better understand these definitions.

Definition of Giftedness	Features
Terman's definition	
Renzulli's definition	
Marland's definition	
Gardner's definition	

2. The Name Game

Person	Time Period	Significant Accomplishments
Charles Darwin		
Sir Francis Galton		
Leta Hollingworth		

Thomas Jefferson		
June Maker		
Sidney Marland		
Joseph Renzulli		
Howard Gardner		
Lewis Terman		

3. Develop your own definition of talent and include a set of criteria to identify children with these abilities.

Definition:

Criteria:

1.

2.

3.

4.

4. In general, there are two different educational approaches to gifted education and there are specific methods used in each approach. List those below.

Approach	Teaching Method
1.	1. 2. 3. 4. 5. 6.
2.	1. 2. 3. 4.

5. Develop a mnemonic to help you remember the teaching methods listed above.

6. Throughout Chapter 7, we discussed a variety of ways that students who are gifted could be identified. Complete the chart to help you analyze these different methods and understand their advantages, disadvantages, and the complexity of the situation.

Means for Identifying Gifted Students

Method	Advantages	Disadvantages
IQ score only		
IQ and creativity test scores		
IQ scores and student work samples		
Teacher and/or community nominations		

7. Some underrepresented subgroups of gifted students were discussed in the chapter. Each group has unique characteristics that often result in these individuals not receiving services. On the next page, summarize these special circumstances or characteristics and provide a resolution to this situation.

Gifted Subgroup	Special Characteristics	Suggested Resolution
Females		
Individuals with disabilities		
Individuals who are culturally and linguistically diverse		

8. Create a web to show the different educational options available to gifted students.

VII. WEB ACTIVITIES

The weblinks for these activities, along with many other resources, can be found at the companion website for the text: www.ablongman.com/smith5e.

1. You have been asked to create a justification for gifted education in your school district. To research your topic and the rationale for the maintenance of special programs for gifted and talented students, identify five web sites that will add interest and various dimensions to your presentation. To start your search, you might try:

    www.us.mensa.org
    www.gifted.org/society
    www.cec.sped.org

2. Gifted education is not supported by IDEA. So, research, demonstration, and training projects are not funded through the federal Office of Special Education Programs, but rather through the U.S. Department of Education's Jacob Javits Programs. Compare the types of projects funded by each of these programs. To do so, you might begin with the home page for the U.S. Department of Education: www.ed.gov

VIII. FOCUS QUESTIONS

1. What is the current vision of giftedness and talent?

2. Regardless of the definition applied, what descriptors can be used for gifted and talented individuals?

3. What factors can inhibit giftedness and talent development?

4. Why are educators concerned about issues related to underrepresentation of some subgroups of gifted learners?

5. What are two major gifted education approaches, and how do they differ from one another?

6. Why, across the history of the United States, has there been such an inconsistent commitment to gifted education?

IX. THINKING ABOUT DILEMMAS TO SOLVE

Consider the following issues. Think broadly about how the dilemmas listed below might be solved in this new century. Remember, no "correct" answers or proven solutions to these problems have been agreed upon (or even tested). Regardless, they are important to students with disabilities and their families.

1. In what ways can gifted and talented students' educational needs be met if special programs are not available?

2. How can identification practices become more flexible, yet not include those who cannot profit from an enriched or accelerated educational program?

3. What should we consider when thinking about whether gifted education is necessary or not?

4. Should gifted education be included in IDEA? Why or why not?

5. Why is there such inconsistent support for gifted education across the years and across locations?

X. PUTTING IT ALL TOGETHER

1. Discussion Questions:

a. How would you study the efficacy and long-term outcomes of gifted education?

b. How would you resolve issues related to the heterogeneity of students – their wide range of skills and abilities – which seems to make meeting all students' educational needs challenging?

c. What are the barriers to the inclusion of more diverse learners in gifted education programs?

d. How can community partners become more involved in school-based programs for gifted, talented, and creative children?

e. What factors might alter girls' under-achievement and under-representation in gifted programs?

2. Mini-case Study

Tommy's case: Tommy is a 10-year old, "twice-exceptional" student. Identified as having exceptional talents in the areas of science and math at the age of five, Tommy has been receiving educational services through various gifted and talented programs for the last five years. During that time he struggled with reading and writing activities. However, his difficulties went virtually undetected as he compensated for the deficits with strong verbal skills and creative projects (i.e., videotaped documentaries rather than written reports). Tommy's learning disability has recently been identified, and he and his parents are about to attend their first meeting to determine his individualized education program.

a. What kinds of educational placements should the special services committee consider for Tommy? What factors must they consider when making placement decisions?

b. What types of instructional methods should be used to address Tommy's reading and writing difficulties? Should these be different than those used to address his talents in math and science?

c. How much should Tommy participate in the decision about his educational program?

d. How can technology be used to enhance Tommy's educational outcomes?

e. Finish Tommy's story.

XI. PUZZLES: A TIME TO PLAY

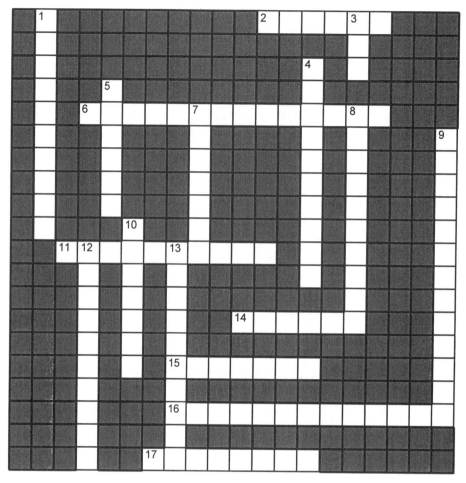

Across

2 Program where students are placed in job settings
4 The ability to produce original ideas, and flexible, detailed responses.
5 Adding topics or skills to traditional curriculum
7 Students with high intelligence, outstanding abilities, and capacity for high performance.
11 Using different language and behavior appropriate in different settings
16 Spurred funding for gifted education
17 Brought attention to gifted students with learning disabilities
18 Programs where gifted students are paired with adults who have similar interests
19 Underrepresented in gifted programs

Down

1 Developed the three-ring concept of giftedness
3 Comprehensive curriculum which incorporates counseling into program
6 Advanced classes for high achieving students
8 Dynasty in which gifted and talented children were educated in the Imperial Court.
9 Mixed ability groups work together
10 Developed the most widely used definitions of gifted and talented
12 Current criticism of gifted programs
13 _____-exceptional
14 Enrichment activities incorporated into general education curriculum
15 Enriched or accelerated activities studied in the general education classroom

XII. MAKING CONNECTIONS
Rent and watch the movie "*Little Man Tate*". Answer the following questions:

1. What was your overall impression of the movie?

2. List five realistic things as well as five unrealistic things about the movie.

	Realistic	Unrealistic
a.		
b.		
c.		
d.		
e.		

3. Do you think the outcome would have been different if the family had been wealthier? Why or why not?

4. Do you think this movie is an accurate portrayal of giftedness and talent development? Why or why not?

SOMETHING TO THINK ABOUT Diverse children are underrepresented in gifted programs.

8

EMOTIONAL OR BEHAVIORAL DISORDERS

People with disabilities do have to face . . . restrictions, . . . but such restrictions are not imposed by their disabilities. They are imposed by a society which discriminates against people with disabilities, creating restrictions by denying people the means to exercise their capabilities. (Sutherland, 1981, p. 22)

I. IMPORTANT POINTS TO REMEMBER

➢ There are two major categories of emotional or behavioral disorders: externalizing and internalizing.

➢ Internalizing behavioral disorders more frequently go unrecognized.

➢ Children who are socially maladjusted are not included in the IDEA definition of emotional disturbance.

➢ Quantifying emotional and behavioral disorders is difficult.

➢ A higher proportion of students with behavioral disorders or emotional disturbance drop out of school.

➢ Eight boys for every girl are identified as having this disability.

II. TIMELINE

Review the timeline presented below. Knowing something about the history of emotional or behavioral disorders might help you understand some of the issues related to students with these disabilities.

1547   St. Mary of Bethlehem (also called Bedlam), the first institution for people with emotional or behavioral disorders, is founded in London.

1700-1800s	Benjamin Rush, father of American psychiatry, proposes humane methods for caring for children with emotional or behavioral disorders.
1841	Dorothea Dix begins a crusade for better care of people with emotional disturbance.
1844	The Association of Medical Superintendents of American Institutions (now called the American Psychiatric Association) is formed.
1871	The first public school class opens for students who were trouble makers in New Haven, Connecticut.
1899	The first juvenile court is established in Chicago.
1908	Clifford Beers publishes *A Mind that Found Itself*.
1909	William Healy begins the Juvenile Psychopathic Institute in Chicago. National Committee for Mental Hygiene is formed.
1924	American Orthopsychiatric Association begins.
1925	House of Refuge, the first institution for juvenile delinquents in the United States, is founded in New York.
1930	White House Conference on Child Health and Protection is held.
1931	Children's Psychiatric Hospital in Rhode Island is established.
1935	Lauretta Bender develops educational services for children at Bellevue Hospital.
1943	Leo Kanner's book, *Child Psychiatry*, stimulates services for children with emotional disturbance.
1944	Bruno Bettelheim begins his work on the "therapeutic milieu" and the Orthogenic School at the University of Chicago.
1960	Nicholas Hobbs of Vanderbilt University initiates Project Re-Ed.
1961	Eli Bower develops a definition of emotional disturbance that is the basis for the federal definition used today.

1962   Norris Haring and Lakin Philips publish *Educating Emotionally Disturbed Children* stressing their theories and applications of the behavioral approach to the education of these students.

1964   The Council for Children with Behavioral Disorders is formed.

1965   Nicholas Long, William Morse, and Ruth Newman publish *Conflict in the Classroom*, a text widely used in colleges and universities to train teachers.

1968   Frank Hewett publishes *The Emotionally Disturbed Child in the Classroom*, and reports his work on the engineered classroom at the Santa Monica Project.

1996   Montrose M. Wolf receives the Father Flanagan Award for Service to Youth for his work in the development of Boys Town's Family Home Program which has served more than one million troubled or at-risk girls and boys.

1997   IDEA removes the term "serious" from this special education category.

III. MAIN IDEAS AND DETAILS

Main Ideas	Details
1.	1. Internalizing 2. 3. Low incidence
2. Prevalence	1. 2. 3.

Main Ideas	Details
3.	1. Schizophrenia 2. Tourette's Syndrome
4. Causes	1. 2. 3. 4.
5.	1. Critical Skills Index 2. 3. Systematic Screening for Behavior Disorders
7. Educational methods	1. 2. 3.
8. Collaboration	1. 2.

Main Ideas	Details
9. Families	1. 2. 3.
10. Technology	1. 2. 3.
11.	1. 2.

IV. DEFINE THESE TERMS

Define these important terms listed below. Remember, if you get stuck, you may use the glossary in the back of your textbook.

ABC Model

anorexia

anxiety disorders

behavioral specific praise

conduct disorders

ecological assessment

emotional disturbance

emotional or behavioral disorders

externalizing behaviors

functional assessments

group contingencies

intervention ladder

positive reinforcement

schizophrenia

self-determination

setting demands

social maladjustment

Tourette's syndrome

wraparound services

V.   ALPHABET SOUP

There are a number of abbreviations used in special education. Identify the following that relate to special education and were discussed in Chapter 8.

ABC

ADHD

BIP

CBM

CDF

CYC

EBD

FAS

VI. STUDY ORGANIZERS

1. There are three major groups of emotional or behavioral disorders: externalizing, internalizing and low incidence. Below, provide some examples of each type.

Externalizing Behaviors	Internalizing Behaviors	Internalizing Behaviors
1.	1.	1.
2.	2.	2.
3.	3.	3.

2. The Name Game

Person	Time Period	Significant Accomplishments
Bruno Bettelheim		
Eli Bower		
Augusta Bronner		
Dorothea Dix		

146

Sigmund Freud		
Samuel Gridley Howe		
Norris Haring		
William Healy		
Frank Hewett		
Nicholas Hobbs		
Leo Kanner		
Jim Kauffman		
Philippe Pinel		
Lakin Phillips		
Benjamin Rush		
Hill Walker		
Montrose Wolf		

3. List the characteristics of emotional or behavioral disorders and explain each of these characteristics in your own words.

Characteristics	Explanation
1.	
2.	
3.	
4.	
5.	

4. List five descriptions that should be included in a BIP.

1.	5.
2.	
3.	
4.	

5. Identify the three tactics discussed in your textbook that are part of the Intervention Ladder and describe how they work.

1.
2.
3.

6. Earlier, you learned about pictorial mnemonics. Use this learning strategy to remember the seven conceptual models used in the treatment of children with emotional or behavioral disorders. When developing a pictorial mnemonic, make up the sentence using the first letter of the important terms, make a mental image of your sentence, and then draw out the picture and the mnemonic so you will remember it better. *(Hint: See Table 8.3 in your text for the names and a review of these models.)*

7. A variety of factors can cause emotional or behavioral disorders. These can be grouped into three major areas. Identify each of the causes and explain specific factors that relate to each causation.

Cause	Factors
1.	1.
2.	2.
3.	3.

VIII. WEB ACTIVITIES

 Everyday, more and more information is posted on the internet. This access to information allows for easier and in-depth study on issues and topics. Learning how to negotiate the internet develops a valuable skill which will assist you as you study and work with students with disabilities and their families. The weblinks for these activities, along with many other resources, can be found at the companion website for the text: www.ablongman.com/smith5e.

1. Use the internet to locate sites that present information about violence in schools and its prevention. After researching this topic, formulate your opinion about the law and students with disabilities who are involved in violent acts at school. Here are some useful sites to begin your research:
   www.aecf.org/kidscount/kc1999/
   www.brt.uoregon.edu
   http://nces.ed.gov/index.html

2. Create a hypothetical case where a student with EBD requires a behavioral intervention plan (BIP). To help you with this task, you might find some useful information at:
   www.pbis.org
   http://maxweber.hunter.cuny.edu/eres/docs/eres?EDSpC715_MCINTYRE/715/HomePage.html
   http://www.ideapractices.org

VIII. FOCUS QUESTIONS

After studying the information presented in the textbook chapter and doing the exercises found in this study guide chapter, you should be able to answer the advance organizer questions listed at the beginning of the textbook chapter. Answer these questions to see if you need to review the material in this workbook and textbook again.

1. Compare the components of the IDEA and National Mental Health and Special Education Coalition definitions.

2. What are the major subgroups of this disability, and how would you describe the conditions that fall into each subgroup?

3. What are the major causes of this disability, and how can it be prevented?

4. What are probable outcomes for these children when effective intervention is not provided?

5. How can teachers help children with this disability?

6. What is the array of educational placement options used for students with emotional or behavioral disorders and how can services be improved?

IX. THINKING ABOUT DILEMMAS TO SOLVE

Consider the following issues. Think broadly about how the dilemmas listed below might be solved in this new century. Remember, no "correct" answers or proven solutions to these problems have been agreed upon (or even tested). Regardless, they are important to students with disabilities and their families.

1. What actions might reduce the overrepresentation of African American boys in the EBD special education category?

2. Why do some schools have better outcomes for students with EBD compared to other schools?

3. What factors could be put into place to increase school attendance, grade point averages, and these students' positive feelings about school?

4. What changes to school programs might serve to decrease the dropout rates of students with EBD?

X. PUTTING IT ALL TOGETHER
1. Discussion Questions:

   a. How might emotional or behavioral disorders be prevented?

   b. What proactive methods and alternative treatment programs could be implemented at inner city, high poverty schools to handle inappropriate behavior?

   c. How might students with disabilities who are in the juvenile justice system be better served?

   d. What should comprise an appropriate education for students with emotional or behavioral disorders?

   e. What agencies could be tapped to develop useful partnerships that would benefit students with emotional and behavioral disorders and their families? How might such partnerships be useful?

   f. What steps could be taken to improve the foster care services offered to students with emotional or behavioral disorders? What other options might be developed for children who need to be removed from their families?

2. Mini-case Study:

Philip's case: Philip is a highly aggressive four-year old. He terrorizes family and neighborhood pets, steals from his brothers and sisters, and will not mind adults.

   a) How serious do you think Philip's problem is?

   b) What steps need to be taken to help Philip?

   c) What steps need to be taken to help Philip's family?

   d) What outcomes do you predict for Philip?

   e) Finish Philip's story.

XI. PUZZLES: A TIME TO PLAY

Across
2 The unofficial name for St. Mary of Bethlehem
6 Behavioral requirements of an environment
11 Used to control behavior: controversial
14 The first step on the Intervention Ladder
15 Controversial word in the IDEA definition
16 Behaviors expressed through social withdrawal
17 A type of internalizing behavior

Down
1 A conceptual model: based on Skinner's work
3 Method of analyzing behavior by looking at antecedent and consequent events
4 All the child's needs are met through collaboration among agencies
5 Developed the engineered classroom
7 Most common form of mistreatment of children
8 Effective _____ can prevent many negative behaviors
9 Aggressive behaviors directed towards others
10 One of the three causal areas of EBD
12 _____ assessment: collected in the student's natural environment
13 A type of externalizing behavior

XII. MAKING CONNECTIONS

The IRIS website is an excellent place to obtain resources on disability. The website also has several modules that are very helpful. Go to http://iris.peabody.vanderbilt.edu/onlinemodules.html and click on to the module about challenging behaviors. Work through the module and answer the questions.

PHYSICAL IMPAIRMENTS AND SPECIAL HEALTH CARE NEEDS

Randy Souders uses a wheelchair and participates in Very Special Arts. He shares his feelings about becoming disabled:

> Everyone, I guess, has this feeling of "Why me?" But all in all, I look back, and I think, "Well, why not me?" What happened to me happens so many thousands of times each year -- especially to young athletic males who are out there playing games, jumping off things, riding bikes and motorcycles. Every year the hospitals fill up with these young boys who've taken a bad spill. Yeah. I felt the anger, the depression. I don't think I ever got to that point where I wanted to end it all. But I was just so -- fed up. (Smith & Plimpton, 1993, p. 148)

I. IMPORTANT POINTS TO REMEMBER

> ➤ This category of special education includes many different groups of students who have a wide range of abilities and disabilities.

> ➤ Many physical impairments and special health care needs are relatively easy to prevent.

> ➤ Many students with physical impairments and special health care needs have multiple disabilities.

> ➤ Motor development, self-help in daily living, and social skills are important instructional targets for students with physical impairments and special health care needs; instruction in these areas should begin during the preschool years.

> ➤ Teachers need to be prepared to deal with medical emergencies and provide for health care in the classroom.

> ➤ Technology can dramatically improve the lives of many individuals with physical impairments and special health care needs.

II. TIMELINE

Review the timeline presented below. Knowing something about the history of special education might help you understand some of the issues related to students with disabilities.

600   Spinal surgery is performed, even though anesthesia and sterile surgical techniques are not available (they did not appear until the 1800s).

1861   William Little, an English surgeon, describes the condition now known as cerebral palsy.

1883   The Industrial School for Crippled and Deformed Children, the first institution for children with physical disabilities, is established in Boston.

1884   The first hospital devoted to children with physical disabilities, Home of the Merciful Savor, was opened in Philadelphia.

1900   The first public school classes for "crippled" children are started in Chicago.

1918   The Soldiers' Rehabilitation Act is passed.

1920   The Citizens' Vocational Rehabilitation Act is passed, providing vocational rehabilitation services to people with physical disabilities.

1921   Franklin D. Roosevelt contracts polio.

1960s   Jonas Salk creates a vaccine to prevent polio.

1965   The National Commission on Architectural Barriers is established to study problems faced by people with physical disabilities.

1973   Section 504 of the Rehabilitation Act is passed to prohibit discrimination against people with physical disabilities.

1977   A wheelchair sit-in is organized in the office of the secretary of the Department of Health, Education, and Welfare; as a result, Section 504 of the Rehabilitation Act is implemented.

1984   Ed Roberts, co-founder of the World Institute on Disabilities, is recognized by the MacArthur Foundation.

1990   The Americans with Disabilities Act—legislation to insure the rights of individuals with disabilities—is signed into law.

1995   Ed Roberts, a catalyst in the civil rights movement of people with disabilities, dies.

1997   IDEA reauthorization lists ADHD as a disability in the "other health impairments" category.

III. MAIN IDEAS AND DETAILS

Main Ideas	Details
1. Physical impairments and special health care needs defined	1. 2.
2.	1. Epilepsy 2. 3.
3. Muscular/skeletal conditions	1. 2.
4. Chronic Illnesses	1. 2.
5. Infectious diseases	1. 2.

Main Ideas	Details
6. Attention Deficit/Hyperactivity Disorder	1. 2. 3. 4.
7. History of the Field	1. 2.
8.	1. ADHD included in health impairment category 2. 3.
9. Causes and Prevention	1. 2. 3. 4.
12. Characteristics	1. 2. 3. 4.

Main Ideas	Details

13. Education
   ➤ Early childhood
   ➤ Elementary through high
     school
	1.
	
	2.
	
	3.
	
	4.
	
	5.

14. Collaboration for inclusion	1. 2.
15. Transition through adulthood	1. 2.
16. Families	1. 2.
17. Technology	1. 2.
18.	1. 2.

IV. DEFINE THESE TERMS

Define these important terms listed below. Remember, if you get stuck, you may use the glossary in the back of your textbook.

absence seizures

accessibility

aquired immunodeficiency syndrome

asthma

ataxia

aura

bionic artificial limbs

blood disorders

cerebral palsy

childhood cancer

chronic illnesses

complex partial seizures

congenital heart defects

contractures

cystic fibrosis

epilepsy

gait training

general tonic-clonic seizures

high -tech devices

human immunodeficiency virus

infectious diseases

juvenile arthritis

limb deficiencies

low-tech devices

orthopedic

medically fragile

muscular/skeletal conditions

neuromotor impairments

neurological impairment

myoelectric limbs

rehabilitation engineering

robotics

seizures

sickle cell anemia

simple partial seizures

technology –dependent children

tuberculosis

universal design

V. ALPHABET SOUP

There are a number of abbreviations used in special education. Identify the following that relate to special education and were discussed in Chapter 9.

ADA

ADHD

AIDS

BOEC

CIC

CMV

CP

HIV

MD

MS

STORCH

TB

VI. STUDY ORGANIZERS

1. Understanding the different types of seizures is important. Use the charts below to test your knowledge of this neurological impairment.

Seizures

Type	Characteristics
1.	
2.	
3.	
4.	

2. List three keys to preventing disabilities.

1.	
2.	
3.	

3. There are three major types of cerebral palsy, as defined by movement. Complete the chart below to better understand each type and how it can affect the individual.

	Type	Impact
1.		
2.		
3.		

4. The Name Game

Person	Time Period	Significant Accomplishments
Hippocrates		
Justin Dart		
Ed Roberts		
Jonas Salk		

5. Major causes and preventive measures for physical impairments are identified in your text. List five of those common causes and indicate how each can be prevented.

Cause	Prevention
1.	
2.	

3.	
4.	
5.	

6. Describe three ways to reduce the impact of absences from school for a child with special health care needs.

1.
2.
3.

7. Technology is extremely important in the lives of many people with physical impairments and special health care needs. Below, identify various kinds of high and low technological advances, and briefly describe their benefits to people with these disabilities.

Low-tech devices	Benefits
High-tech devices	Benefits

VII. WEB ACTIVITIES

Everyday, more and more information is posted on the internet. This access to information allows for easier and in-depth study on issues and topics. Learning how to negotiate the internet develops a valuable skill which will assist you as you study and work with students with disabilities and their families. The weblinks for these activities, along with many other resources, can be found at the companion website for the text: www.ablongman.com/smith5e.

1. A group of friends, some with and some without disabilities, have asked you to help them plan a trip to an exciting place for their two-week vacation. The vacation spot you select must be accessible to people who use wheelchairs. Come up with several suggestions and be able to describe their choices. One place to start your search is: www.gimponthego.com

2. Organizations such as the Shake-a-Leg organization provide mainstream recreational therapeutic services that develop independent living skills for individuals who have experienced spinal cord injury and related nervous system disorders. Use their web site, or find another, to describe to a family of a child with severe physical impairments to wide range of recreational activities that are available: www.shakealeg.org

VIII. FOCUS QUESTIONS

After studying the information presented in the textbook chapter and doing the exercises found in this study guide chapter, you should be able to answer the advance organizer questions listed at the beginning of the textbook chapter. Answer these questions to see if you need to review the material in this workbook and textbook again.

1. How are physical impairment and special healthcare needs classified and organized?

2. What are some steps teachers should follow to assist a child who is having a seizure?

3. What are the different types of cerebral palsy?

4. How can the learning environment be modified to accommodate students with physical impairments and special health care needs?

5. How do students with ADHD qualify for special education services?

6. What are the barriers to the full participation of these individuals in society, and how can they be minimized?

IX. THINKING ABOUT DILEMMAS TO SOLVE

Consider the following issues. Think broadly about how the dilemmas listed below might be solved in this new century. Remember, no "correct" answers or proven solutions to these problems have been agreed upon (or even tested). Regardless, they are important to students with disabilities and their families.

1. How can the educational system better respond to the needs of students with physical disabilities or special health care needs?

2. Why do some states use separate special education schools for students with physical disabilities while others do not?

3. What is the impact of fully including all medically fragile students in general education classrooms on those directly involved?

4. What might be the implications of including ADHD as a condition under the health impairments category?

5. How should teachers be prepared to work with children with these special needs?

X. PUTTING IT ALL TOGETHER
   1. Discussion questions:

a) How might general education teachers be better prepared to meet the needs of students with physical disabilities or special health care needs?

b) What should be done about older buildings and facilities that are not fully accessible?

c) Should the federal government have a role in the prevention of disabilities on a national level, as it did with the Vaccines for Children's Program? Should that role be permanent and expanded or should it be left to each state to develop such programs?

d) Should costs of services weigh in when decisions are being made about the types and intensities of special education supports provided to students with disabilities? Explain your thinking on this issue.

e) School district officials often say that budget restrictions do not allow for availability of school nurses at every school; however, teachers and parents are concerned about the handling of some very special health care needs in classroom settings without nurses' help. How might this dilemma be solved?

2. Mini-case Study:

   In previous chapters, you were presented with mini-case studies. Using those as samples, create your own mini-case study for a child with a physical impairment or a special health care need. Write the mini-case study, answer the questions, write some additional questions of your own, and answer them.

   The Child's Case:

   a) What special accommodations might the school need to make for this child?

   b) In what special ways should the teacher work with this child's family?

   c)

   d)

   f) Finish the story.

XI. PUZZLES: A TIME FOR PLAY

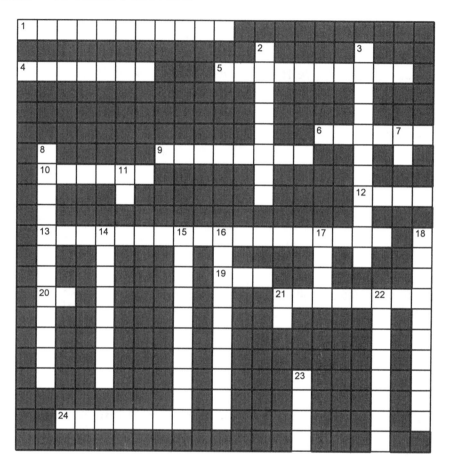

Across

1 Spinal column has not closed properly
4 _____ illness: Sick for long periods of time
5 Prenatal care and vaccinations are examples of this
6 A group of infectious diseases
9 _____ arthritis
10 Most common chronic illness in children
12 Signals an impending seizure
13 Contagious: HIV, AIDS, and STORCH infections are examples of this
19 A type of STORCH infection (abbr.)
20 Tuberculosis (abbr.)
21 _____/skeletal condition
24 A type of CP: uncontrolled tightening or pulling of muscles

Down

2 One cause of physical disabilities
3 One of the first to treat physical impairments
7 Cerebral palsy (abbr.)
8 Preventive technique
11 Rare, incurable disease which weakens and destroys muscles (abbr.)
14 A condition with recurrent seizures
15 _____ impairment: IDEA condition related to a physical deformity
16 Hereditary blood disorder
17 Incurable syndrome caused by infection of the immune system
18 _____ impairment: involving nerves, muscles, and motor functioning
21 Disease typically affecting adults (abbr.)
22 Most common form of childhood cancer
23 Developed the polio vaccine

VII. MAKING CONNECTIONS

Pretend for a day that you are paralyzed from your waist down. Using a wheelchair, complete the below assignment and then answer the questions that follow.
- ➤ Meet some friends for lunch at a restaurant.
- ➤ Go grocery shopping.
- ➤ Go shopping for some clothes in a mall.

1. Which of the assignments was the most difficult and why?

2. How did people react to you?

10

DEAFNESS OR HARD OF HEARING

Mary Herring Wright's memoirs reveal a unique perspective of a Black, Deaf girl growing up segregated in two important ways by mainstream American culture. She writes of her mixed feelings about leaving the comfort of familiar people and surroundings after graduating from the Black School for the Deaf in North Carolina, to pursue her dream.

> My deafness hadn't bothered me in the past but now I thought of so many things -- the way I was politely passed over when someone in the church wanted something done, the quick snicker when I misunderstood something said to me, and the other little things. If it was like that among people who knew me, what it would be like without Mama or someone here at school to make me feel like I was a person too? Then I thought of what Mama always told me: I was just as intelligent as anyone else and could do anything the rest could do; I should hold my head up and be proud; I shouldn't get angry or feel hurt because of a few laughs at my mistakes....I wanted to help with the war somehow....I wanted to work with Uncle Sam, but did Uncle Sam want me? (Wright, 1999, pps. 274-275)

In 1942, Ms. Wright began working for the Department of the Navy. In 1950, she married. She has four daughters. One works for Gallaudet, one is a lawyer, one an artist, and one a housewife.

I. IMPORTANT POINTS TO REMEMBER

> ➢ Even mild hearing losses (15 dB) can be educationally significant.

> ➢ Individuals whose hearing loss occurs after the age of three (after the development of language) retain abilities to communicate orally.

> ➢ Almost all deaf individuals perceive some sound.

> ➢ Hearing loss in children is the number one birth defect.

> ➢ The leading causes of deafness in schoolchildren are meningitis and heredity.

> ➢ Children whose hearing loss are detected before 6 months old tend to have better outcomes than those detected later.

> ➢ The sooner intervention programs begin for these students and their families, the better.

> ➢ The academic achievement of deaf students is usually quite low, with reading being the greatest problem.

> ➢ Students who are hard of hearing tend to be quite different from those who are deaf in the areas of speech intelligibility, academic achievement, and usefulness of hearing aids.

> ➢ Technological advances have and continue to make a significant impact on the lives of those who are deaf, but such equipment is expensive and often out of the economic reach of these individuals.

II. TIMELINE

Review the timeline presented below. Knowing something about the history of deafness or hearing loss might help you understand some of the issues related to students with these disabilities.

1500s	Pedro Ponce, a Spanish monk, is the first teacher of students who were deaf, and has remarkable success in teaching them to read, write, and speak.
1600s	William Holder and John Wallis begin deaf education programs in England.
1775	Michel de l'Epee starts the first school for deaf children in Paris.
1776	Samuel Heinicke starts the first state-supported school in Germany for students who were deaf.
1817	The first school in the United States — the American Asylum for the Education of the Deaf and Dumb (now the American School for the Deaf) — for deaf students is started in Hartford, Connecticut, by Thomas Hopkins Gallaudet.
1817	Laurent Clerc (father of the education of the deaf in the U.S.) comes to America from France advocating the use of manual communication.
1864	By this time, 24 schools for the deaf are in operation.

| 1864 | Gallaudet University (first called the National Deaf Mute College) is founded. |

| 1883 | Alexander Graham Bell and Edward Gallaudet's debates about how people who were deaf should live and be educated reach a peak. |

| 1958 | PL 85-905 provides funding for captioned films for the deaf. |

| 1965 | PL 89-258 amends the Captioned Films for the Deaf Act and enacts the National Advisory Committee on the Education of the Deaf. |

| 1965 | The National Technical Institute for the Deaf is established by PL 89-36. |

| 1966 | The Model Secondary School for the Deaf is established at Gallaudet through PL 89-694. |

| 1960s | Roy Holcomb develops an approach, the total communication method, that combines the oral and manual communication systems. |

| 1970 | The Kendall Elementary Demonstration School is established at Gallaudet through PL 91-587. |

| 1988 | I. King Jordon becomes the first deaf person to assume the presidency of Gallaudet University. |

| 1988 | Commission on the Education of the Deaf recommends to Congress that the general education classroom not be interpreted as least restrictive for deaf students. |

| 1993 | Closed caption decoders are required components of all television sets sold in America. |

III. MAIN IDEAS AND DETAILS

Organize your notes efficiently by listing the *Main Ideas* in one column and relating at least two *Details* to each main idea. The table below was designed to help you organize your thoughts as you study this chapter in your textbook. To assist you, we provided either the *Main Ideas* or parts of the *Details*. Extra room has been provided to add additional topics for you to remember as you study.

Main Ideas	Details
1. Definitions	1. 2.
2.	1. Conductive hearing loss 2.
3. Identification	1. 2.
4. Causes	1. 2. 3. 4. Maternal rubella 5.
5. Prevention	1. 2. 3. Increased public awareness

Main Ideas	Details
6. Characteristics	1. 2. 3. 4.
7.	1. 2. 3. Cued speech 4.
8.	1. Least restrictive environment 2.
9. Transition through adulthood	1. 2.
10.	1. Assistive devices 2. 3. 4.

Main Ideas	Details
11.	1. 2.

IV. DEFINE THESE TERMS:

Define these important terms listed below. Remember, if you get stuck, you may use the glossary in the back of your textbook.

air conduction audiometry method

alerting devices

American Sign Language

assistive listening devices

assistive devices

audiogram

audio loop

audiometer

behind the ear

bilingual-bicultural approach

bone conduction audiometry method

C-Print

captions

closed captions

cochlear implant

conductive hearing loss

cued speech

Deaf culture

deafness

Deaf pride

decibel

decoder

educational interpreters

finger spelling

FM transmission device

frequency of sound

Gallaudet University

hair cells

hard of hearing

hearing aid

hearing threshold

hertz

in the canal

in the ear

inner ear

manual communication

meningitis

middle ear

open captions

oral-only approach

otoacoustic emissions

outer ear

postlingually deaf

prelingually deaf

pure sounds

real-time translations

sensorineural hearing loss

universal infant screening

Telecoil

telecommunications relay service

text telephone

total communication approach

voice-carry over

V. ALPHABET SOUP

There are a number of abbreviations used in special education. Identify the following that relate to special education and were discussed in Chapter 10.

ABI

ASL

ALDs

ASR

BTE

CIC

CMV

dB

DOD

FM

Hz

ITC

ITE

LRE

NTID

Rh

RTC

SLP

TRS

TTY

VCO

SOMETHING TO THINK ABOUT Deaf babies babble with their hands.

VI. STUDY ORGANIZERS

1. By completing the table below, you should come to understand some important differences between the two types of hearing loss.

Differences Between Two Types of Hearing Loss

	Conductive	Sensorineural
Location		
Assessment		
Correction		
Instruction		

SOMETHING TO THINK ABOUT The Deaf are a minority group.

2. By completing the table below, you should come to understand some important differences between students who are prelingually deaf and those who are postlingually deaf.

Difference Between Prelingual and Postlingual Hearing Loss

	Prelingual	Postlingual
Causation		
Academic achievement		
Communication preference		
Speech abilities		

3. The Name Game

Person	Time Period	Significant Accomplishments
Henry Baker		
Laurent Clerc		
Robert Weitbrecht		

Person	Time Period	Significant Accomplishments
Edward Gallaudet		
Alexander Graham Bell		
William Holder/ John Wallis		
Thomas Hopkins Gallaudet		
I. King Jordan		
Horace Mann		
Charles Michel de L'Epée		
Cynthia Neese Bailes		
Pedro Ponce de Leon		

4. Earlier in the main idea you listed the four basic approaches that are used with deaf students. List them again, define, and summarize the advantages and disadvantages of each approach.

Method	Definition	Advantage/Disadvantage
1.		
2.		
3.		
4.		

5. Technology is particularly important to individuals with severe hearing loss. The four major categories of technology used by many deaf individuals are found on the table below. To test your knowledge of this content, complete the table.

Technological category	Summary/Examples	Use
Assistive Listening Devices (ALDs)		
Telecommunication Devices		
Computerized Speech-to-Text Translations		
Alerting devices		

6. Many different adjustments can be made to the general classroom setting to better accommodate hard-of-hearing students. List some of those below.

Accommodations	Example
1.	
2.	

3.	
Accomodations	Example
5.	
6.	

VII. WEB ACTIVITIES

 Everyday, more and more information is posted on the internet. This access to information allows for easier and in-depth study on issues and topics. Learning how to negotiate the internet develops a valuable skill which will assist you as you study and work with students with disabilities and their families. The weblinks for these activities, along with many other resources, can be found at the companion website for the text: www.ablongman.com/smith5e.

1. Self Help for Hard of Hearing People is an organization that provides a wealth of information for those who having hearing losses. Check out the technology section and see if there are new technology not listed in the textbook chapter. www.shhh.org

2. The Gallaudet Research Institute studies many issues about deaf youngsters' academic achievement and their outcomes as adults. Check out some of their most recent work, and compare these new findings to those reported in your text. To get a link to Gallaudent Research Institute, you can begin from this site: www.gallaudet.edu

VIII. FOCUS QUESTIONS

After studying the information presented in the textbook chapter and doing the exercises found in this study guide chapter, you should be able to answer the advance organizer questions listed at the beginning of the textbook chapter. Answer these questions to see if you need to review the material in this workbook and textbook again.

1. What variables are used to create different subgroups of students who are deaf or hard of hearing?

2. What is meant by the concept of Deaf culture?

3. What are the major causes of hearing loss?

4. Why is universal screening of newborns such an important issue?

5. How do the major instructional methods for deaf children differ, and how should an individual child's communication style affect the choice of instructional method?

6. What types of technology are available to assist the deaf and what advances might the future hold?

IX. THINKING ABOUT DILEMMAS TO SOLVE

Consider the following issues. Think broadly about how the dilemmas listed below might be solved in this new century. Remember, no "correct" answers or proven solutions to these problems have been agreed upon (or even tested). Regardless, they are important to students with disabilities and their families.

1. Should deafness receive special status like other historically underrepresented groups do in the U.S.?

2. What services should deaf children of hearing parents receive?

3. How can the underachievement and poor employment outcomes of many deaf and hard of hearing people be overcome?

4. What must happen for all infants' hearing to be tested?

X. PUTTING IT ALL TOGETHER

1. Discussion Questions:

   a. Should deaf infants receive cochlear implants? What are the issues embedded in this controversy and how should they be resolved?

b. What actions must be taken to improve attitudes and expectations of teachers, administrators, and the public by publicizing the abilities and skills that deaf and hard of hearing individuals can and do achieve?

c. How can we make early intervention programs more consistently available and used by children with disabilities and their families?

d. What steps will need to be taken to ensure high quality preschool programs to students with disabilities?

e. How should the controversies surrounding cochlear implants and young deaf children be resolved?

2. Mini-case Study:

The purpose of the mini-case studies presented in this study guide is to help you extend your knowledge to application situations. There is no single answer to any of the mini-cases, but you should make notes to yourself about how you would support and justify your answer.

Juan's Case: Juan is six years old and was born with a profound congenital hearing loss. He is deaf, but his parents and the rest of his family members hear. Juan lives in a rural community that is quite remote. Since his profound hearing loss was diagnosed several years ago, Juan and his family have spent time at his state's school for the deaf where they have been learning sign language and other special techniques to help Juan learn to communicate. Juan's parents have met with administrators in the local school district to discuss the educational program that could be developed for Juan. If Juan stays at home with his family and attends the local public school, he will receive services from an itinerant teacher of the deaf once a week and his general education teacher will receive consultative services as well. If Juan goes to the residential school, he will attend classes where all of his classmates are deaf, the teachers are specially trained, and he will learn to use the most advanced technology available. This center school is over 200 miles from Juan's home, but the school will arrange for him to come home on most weekends. Juan is from a very close family, and the decision about where Juan should go to school is a difficult one to make.

    a. What factors should Juan's parents consider as they make the decision about his educational placement?

    b. Who should be involved in making this decision?

    c. What should be included in Juan's IEP if he attends his local public school?

    d. How might his IEP differ if he attends a center school?

    e. Finish the story.

XI. PUZZLES: A TIME TO PLAY

Across

1 Unit of measure for sound frequency
3 Uses a pure-tone generator to test for hearing loss
6 The hammer, anvil, and stirrup together make this
9 Some say that this is not the general education classroom
10 Part of inner ear containing fluid and hairlike nerve cells
14 Assistive listening device (abbr.)
15 Type of hearing aid: behind the ear (abbr.)
16 _____ devices: Make individuals aware of events or sounds
19 Method of testing for conductive hearing loss
20 Part of ear where sound waves fall
23 Type of hearing aid: in the ear (abbr.)
25 Electronic microprocessor that replaces the cochlea
26 A type of communication using both oral and manual communication
28 Sound waves of specific frequencies used to test hearing
30 Cause of hearing loss; genetic

Down

1 Another name for the malleus
2 Hearing loss occurs before language development
4 Type of hearing aid: in the canal (abbr.)
5 The language of the Deaf community (abbr.)
7 One of the 3 tiny bones in the middle ear
8 A TTY that allows both voice and text use (abbr.)
11 Subtitles
12 The only accredited liberal arts university for deaf students
13 Enough residual hearing to comprehend oral communication with the help of a hearing aid
17 Disease which causes hearing loss
18 The incus
21 Real-time translations (abbr.)
22 Using the hands to communicate
24 Loud sounds which can cause hearing loss
27 Text telephone (abbr.)
29 Unit of measure for sound intensity

Use the clues given below to find key terms in the word search puzzle. Have fun!

O	I	L	J	G	N	I	R	A	E	H	F	O	D	R	A	H
N	R	N	I	N	T	E	R	P	R	E	T	E	R	S	F	D
V	O	A	C	C	U	E	D	S	P	E	E	C	H	F	E	W
V	A	I	L	U	D	B	Q	M	T	W	J	B	H	A	R	L
Y	U	B	T	O	S	P	D	V	A	A	H	S	F	E	C	A
L	D	I	M	C	N	Y	S	T	H	U	T	N	V	S	E	R
L	I	L	B	K	E	L	N	U	U	A	E	R	H	M	V	U
A	O	I	A	S	E	T	Y	J	P	S	E	H	B	Q	I	E
U	M	N	E	K	Z	Q	E	E	S	N	D	W	S	X	T	N
G	E	G	D	J	R	Z	S	D	Y	J	M	H	W	P	C	I
N	T	U	A	X	Z	R	S	R	Y	A	Y	O	W	E	U	R
I	E	A	C	R	P	U	O	M	T	L	L	E	T	S	D	O
L	R	L	W	D	E	T	D	E	U	S	R	L	D	Y	N	S
T	X	V	L	L	I	O	N	L	T	H	P	A	E	H	O	N
S	C	T	L	D	Z	Q	K	Q	Q	P	V	Q	E	B	C	E
O	V	A	U	A	U	D	I	O	G	R	A	M	K	V	U	S
P	M	A	O	T	I	T	I	S	M	E	D	I	A	H	U	R

1. Grid used to display hearing abilities
2. Instrument used for measuring hearing
3. Carries messages from ear to brain
4. ASL is considered native language and English is second language
5. Hearing loss in outer or middle ear
6. Hand signals that accompany difficult to see oral speech sounds
7. Inability to perceive sounds, with/without hearing aid
8. A key factor in prevention
9. Enough residual hearing to comprehend oral communication with a hearing aid
10. Anvil
11. Related service providers; translators
12. Hammer
13. Method of communication using oral language only
14. Middle ear infection; cause of hearing loss
15. Hearing loss occurs after language development
16. German measles; cause of hearing loss
17. Hearing loss in inner ear
18. Stirrup

XII. MAKING CONNECTIONS

Sometimes the easiest way to understand the ramifications of a disability is to experience it for yourself. Experience the difficulties of a hearing impairment by wearing tight fitting earplugs while having dinner with friends at a restaurant. Answer the following questions:

a. Were you able to keep up with the conversations?

b. What factors, other than the earplugs, kept you from hearing everything?

c. Were there things you or others could have done to help you to participate in the conversations fully?

d. Did you find yourself relying on expressions and hand movements of others to fully understand conversation? If so, why do you think this occurred?

e. Did your experience give you an insight on what accommodations would be helpful in the classroom for students with hearing impairment? If so, list your insights.

11

LOW VISION AND BLINDNESS

Blindness is not just a nuisance like being left-handed in a right-handed world. It is not just an inconvenience like living in a suburb without the ability to drive. What blindness is - and I include a severe visual impairment in this definition as well - is a serious psychological, physiological and cognitive blow to the individual which, left untended, impedes and can even destroy any chance for a normal and productive life.

Have we, in our drive to convince others that blind people are just like everyone else, encouraged (even if unwittingly) the planting of seeds which will ultimately keep blind people from being like everyone else?

I think so. (Gallagher, 1988, p. 227).

I. IMPORTANT POINTS TO REMEMBER

➢ The vast majority of individuals with low vision and blindness use vision as their primary mode for learning.

➢ Early identification is important for both educational and medical reasons.

➢ People with low vision and blindness are not endowed with more acute hearing or tactile senses; these must be developed.

➢ Only between 2% and 4% of blind adults use seeing eye dogs.

➢ Fewer and fewer individuals who are legally blind use braille as their primary reading mode.

➢ General education classrooms often need to be adapted somewhat to accommodate students with severe visual disabilities.

➢ Technological advances, particularly microcomputer technology and speech synthesizers can make any printed information readily accessible to those who can read enlarged print.

II. TIMELINE

Review the timeline presented below. Knowing something about the history of low vision and blindness might help you understand some of the issues related to students with disabilities.

1784   Valentin Haüy begins school (Institution des Jeunes Aveugles) in Paris for students who are blind.

1791   The first school for blind in England opens in Liverpool.

1827   The first federal legislation concerning Americans who are blind provides land in Florida and Kentucky for facilities.

1829   Louise Braille adapts French military code for night communication for persons who were blind (first called sonography).

1829   The New England Asylum for the Blind opens in Watertown, Massachusetts; now called Perkins Institute and Massachusetts School for the Blind.

1832-33 Residential schools for children who are blind opens in New York, Boston, and Philadelphia.

1837   Ohio becomes the first state to make public provision for the education of children with visual disabilities; Ohio State School for the Blind established.

1858   American Printing House for the Blind (APH) is established by the Kentucky state legislature.

1862   A simple means of testing visual acuity using a chart with the letter "E" written in different sizes facing different directions is developed by Snellen, a Dutch ophthalmologist.

1871   The American Association of Instructors for the Blind, now called the The Association for Education and Rehabilitation of the Blind and Visually Impaired (AER), is founded.

1871   Samuel Gridley Howe advocates integration of students who are blind in general education programs.

1877   Thomas Edison invents the phonograph.

1879	Congress passes PL 45-186 to promote educational programs for students who are blind; this act provides the first federal subsidy to provide braille books to persons who are blind and provides an annual appropriation to the American Printing House for the Blind.
1887	Anne Sullivan begins teaching Helen Keller.
1892	The braille typewriter is invented by Frank Hall.
1899	The first law requiring vision testing of school children is passed in Connecticut.
1900	The first class for children who are blind in a regular public school opens in Chicago.
1906	The first radio broadcast occurs in the United States
1909	Robert Irwin organizes braille reading classes in Cleveland public schools.
1913	Roxbury, Massachusetts, and Cleveland, Ohio, institute sight-saving classes.
1918	The University of California institutes a teacher training program for teachers of the blind.
1921	The American Foundation for the Blind is founded.
1928	Seeing-eye dogs are introduced in America.
1931	The Library of Congress begins to distribute braille reading material.
1934	The first talking books on long playing records are produced.
1941	A growing incidence of blindness in infants from ROP is noted.
1947	Hoover cane is developed.
1963-65	A rubella epidemic causes blindness in 5,000–6,000 infants whose mother's had contracted the disease.
1964	Natalie Barraga proves that sight saving classes are ineffective.
1966	The laser cane, which emits beams of light to detect objects, is invented.

1971   The Optacon, a tactual reading machine that changes print into letter configurations, is marketed.

1974   The first CCTV is developed.

1975   The first version of the Kurzweil Reader, which translates printed material into synthesized speech, is invented.

1997   IDEA requires that braille be considered as a reading option for all blind students, and must be addressed in the student's IEP.

III. MAIN IDEAS AND DETAILS

Main Ideas	Details
1. Visual disabilities defined	1. 2. 3.
2.	1. Low vision 2. Blindness
3.	1. 2. Adventitiously blind
4. Causes and prevention	1. 2. 3.

Main Ideas	Details
5.	1. Inappropriate social behaviors 2.
6. Early childhood education	1. 2.
7.	1. 2. Printed materials 3.
8. Orientation and mobility	1. 2. 3.
9. Accommodations	1. 2. 3.
10. Transition through adulthood	1. 2.

Main Ideas	Details
11.	1. 2. Audio imput- Talking books 3.
12.	1. 2.

IV. DEFINE THESE TERMS:

Define these important terms listed below. Remember, if you get stuck, you may use the glossary in the back of your textbook.

accommodation

advance organizers

adventitiously blind

analytic listening

appreciative listening

attentive listening

audiodescription

blindness

braille

central vision

closed-circuit television

congenitally blind

cornea

distance senses

guide dogs

Hoover cane

iris

Kurzweil Reader

legally blind

lens

life skills

long cane

low vision

marginal listening

mobility

multiple disabilities

ophthalmologist

optician

optic nerve

optometrist

orientation

outreach programs

peripheral vision

personal reader

pupil

residual vision

retina

selective listening

Snellen chart

sound localization

tactile maps

talking books

tunnel vision

visual acuity

visual efficiency

V. ALPHABET SOUP

There are a number of abbreviations used in special education. Identify the following that relate to special education and were discussed in Chapter 10.

ADA

CCTV

ROP

SOMETHING TO THINK ABOUT Proportionally few children, when compared to people over the age of 65, have severe low vision or blindness.

VI. STUDY ORGANIZERS

1. To understand how the visual process works, it is important to be able to trace the actions that must occur for an individual to see. Use the box below to make a sketch of the vision process (see Figure 11.1 in your textbook). Then, label the names of the parts of the eye. Also, talk to yourself as you describe how vision occurs.

2. People with visual disabilities have various reading preferences. Completing the table below should help you know and understand these different reading styles.

Reading Preference	Description	Advantages/Disadvantages
braille		
Enlarged Print		
Computer Synthesized Voice		
Personal Readers		
Audio Recordings		

3. The Name Game

Person	Time Period	Significant Accomplishments
Edward Allen		
Louis Braille		

Person	Time Period	Significant Accomplishments
Thomas Edison		
Samuel Gridley Howe		
Frank Hall		
Valentine Haüy		
Richard Hoover		
Robert Irwin		

VII. WEB ACTIVITIES

Everyday, more and more information is posted on the internet. This access to information allows for easier and in-depth study on issues and topics. Learning how to negotiate the internet develops a valuable skill which will assist you as you study and work with students with disabilities and their families. The weblinks for these activities, along with many other resources, can be found at the companion website for the text: www.ablongman.com/smith5e.

1. Develop a public relations campaign to inform general education teachers about the needs of all students with visual disabilities. Include a bulleted list of topics that should be included in the curriculum for all low vision and blind students, regardless of their placement. Here are several websites to get you started:
    www.afb.org
    www.cec.sped.org
    www.aph.org

2. You have been appointed to a task force that will develop a community-service advertising agenda to inform the public about how blindness can be prevented. Develop a list of topics that should be included in the ad series. Here's a good starting place: www.preventblindness.org

VIII. FOCUS QUESTIONS

After studying the information presented in the textbook chapter and doing the exercises found in this study guide chapter, you should be able to answer the advance organizer questions listed at the beginning of the textbook chapter. Answer these questions to see if you need to review the material in this workbook and textbook again.

1. How can the category of visual disabilities be divided into subgroups?

2. What are the major causes of visual disabilities?

3. What are some ways the learning environment can be modified to accommodate students with visual disabilities?

4. Why must orientation and mobility be long-term curriculum targets for many low vision and most blind students, and what specific skills must be included?

5. What technological advances can assist people with visual disabilities at school, in the workplace, and in independent living?

6. Why has braille literacy become such an emotionally charged debate, and how do you think it should be resolved?

IX. THINKING ABOUT DILEMMAS TO SOLVE

Consider the following issues. Think broadly about how the dilemmas listed below might be solved in this new century. Remember, no "correct" answers or proven solutions to these problems have been agreed upon (or even tested). Regardless, they are important to students with disabilities and their families.

1. What strategies might school districts use to meet the IDEA mandate of offering braille instruction to those who need it when there are insufficient numbers of teachers available who know how to teach this skill to students?

2. What can be done to raise the literacy levels of blind and low vision students who read print?

3. What are some ways to eliminate bias and discrimination experienced by people with visual disabilities?

4. Think about ways instruction in life skills can be provided to students with visual disabilities who are participating fully in the general education curriculum.

5. Devise methods of improving employment rates for this group of people.

X. PUTTING IT ALL TOGETHER

1. Discussion Questions:

   a. What methods should be employed to educate all teachers about the needs of students with visual disabilities, even those who have benefited from new technologies and medical treatments to reduce the impact of their visual loss?

b. What guidelines should be developed to assist parents, educators, and students with visual disabilities in balancing the benefits and liabilities ("trade offs") inherent in placement decisions?

c. How can educators ensure that specialized instruction in orientation and mobility is sufficiently available to students with visual disabilities who attend general education settings?

d. How might both special education and general education teachers better learn to systematically instruct and guide opportunities that facilitate the development of good social interaction abilities in blind and low vision students?

2. Mini case-study

Susanne's case: You are a special educator attending an IEP meeting where the decision about the instructional program and educational placement of Susanne, a blind student, will be discussed. You need to prepare fully for this meeting to ensure Susanne's life skills, mobility, and literacy needs are met. Susanne has been attending her neighborhood elementary school, and it is now time for transition to middle school. Susanne has expressed concerns about the way many of her classmates treat her, she feels excluded from her peer group in part because she has not fully developed independent mobility skills. As with all blind students, her IEP must address access to braille instruction. To assist her parents in making decisions about placement and instruction, help them consider all aspects of her educational program.

a. How would you prepare for this IEP meeting?

b. Make a checklist of points that need to be discussed at the IEP meeting.

c. Who else should be in attendance at this meeting?

d. What role should Susanne have at her IEP meeting?

e. What placement options should be considered?

e. Finish the story.

XI. PUZZLES: A TIME TO PLAY

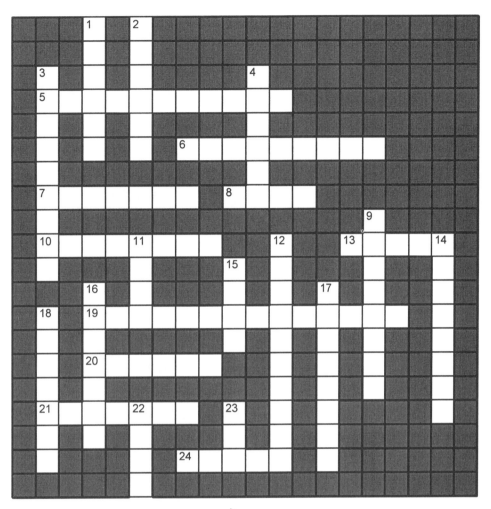

Across

5 Mental map used to move through environments
6 No functional sight
7 Chart used to test vision
8 Hoover _____
10 Person who fills eyeglass or corrective lense prescriptions
13 Greek poet who was blind
19 Visual impairment acquired after age two
20 Inside lining of the eye
21 Visual acuity at 20/200 or worse
24 Lets light into the eye

Down

1 Visual _____: How well a person can see at distances
2 _____ vision: Limitation in peripheral vision
3 Level of impairment where vision is still useful
4 Transparent, curved part of eye
9 Ability to travel safely from one point to another
11 Television used for transmissions (abbr.)
12 Outer area of visual field
14 _____ vision: Amount of vision despite visual disability
15 Colored part of the eye
16 Discovered that vision can worsen if not used
17 Animals that help with mobility
18 Reading and writing using raised dots
22 Brings objects into focus
23 Retinopathy of prematurity (abbr.)

XII. MAKING CONNECTIONS

Draw a diagram in the space below of how a classroom should be arranged to accommodate a student with a low vision impairment or blindness.

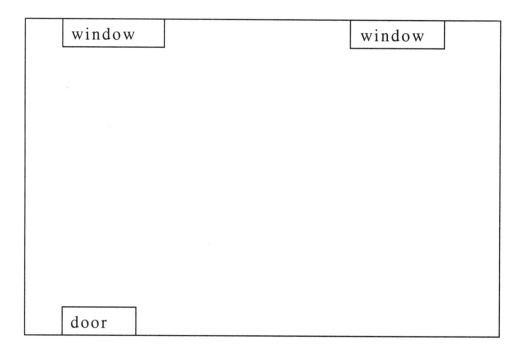

12

AUTISTIC SPECTRUM DISORDERS

I.   IMPORTANT POINTS TO REMEMBER

> ➤ Diagnosis as early as before three years of age is now possible.

> ➤ Autism exists from very early childhood.

> ➤ Many different causes for autism have been proposed, and today definitive answers are still unavailable although it is known to be neurological in origin.

> ➤ The rate of autistic spectrum disorders is rising.

II. TIMELINE
Review the timeline presented below. Knowing something about the history of special education might help you understand some of the issues related to students with disabilities.

1943	Leo Kanner coins the term "autism."
1961	The National Society for Autistic Children is formed.
1965	Bernard Rimland begins his study of autism.
1990	Autism becomes a separate special education category, according to the 1997 reauthorization of IDEA.
1995	Temple Grandin publishes her autobiography describing her life with autism, and broadens people's conception of the autism spectrum.

III. MAIN IDEAS AND DETAILS

Organize your notes efficiently by listing the *Main Ideas* in one column and relating at least two *Details* to each main idea. The table below was designed to help you organize your thoughts as you study this chapter in your textbook. To assist you, we provided either the *Main Ideas* or parts of the *Details*. Extra room has been provided to add additional topics for you to remember as you study.

Main Ideas	Details
1.	1. Autism 2. Asperger's Disorder 3. Rett's Syndrome 4. Childhood Disintegrative Disorder 5. Pervasive Developmental Disability
2. Areas affected by Autistic Spectrum Disorders	1. 2. 3.
3.	1. 2. dramatic increase in autism
4. Causes	1. 2. 3. 4.

Main Ideas	Details
5.	1. No specific physical features 2. Present from birth or very early in the developmental period 3.
6. Early childhood education	1. 2. 3.
7. Elementary through high school	1. 2. 3. 4.
8.	1. sufficient structure 2. supports for functional communication 3. 4.

9. Transition through adulthood	1. 2. 3.
10.	1. 2. 3. Picture Exchange Communication System
11.	1. 2. 3.
12.	1. 2. 3.

IV. DEFINE THESE TERMS:

Define these important terms listed below. Remember, if you get stuck, you may use the glossary in the back of your textbook.

Asperger's syndrome

autism

autistic disorder

autistic spectrum disorder

autistic savants

childhood disintegrative disorder

echolalia

joint attention

pervasive development disorder – not
otherwise specified

Picture Exchange Communications System

Rett's syndrome

stereotypic behaviors

structured teaching

Young Autism Program

V. ALPHABET SOUP

There are a number of abbreviations used in special education. Identify the following that relate to autistic spectrum disorders and were discussed in Chapter 12.

ADOS

ABA

ACC

AIT

ASD

CARS

CDD

CHAT

DSM-IV

LEAP

PDD-NOS

PECS

STAT

TEAACH

YAP

VI. STUDY ORGANIZERS

1. The Name Game

Person	Significant Accomplishments
Hans Asperger	
Temple Grandin	
Andreas Rhett	
Julie Osterling/ Gerry Dawson	

Helen Keller	
Leo Kanner	
Eugen Bluer	
I. Ovar Lovaas	
Bernard Rimland	

2. Types of ASD

In the *Main Ideas,* the five types of ASD were identified. In the chart below, list the type of ASD, the ways each type is similar and different in comparison to the other types.

Type	Similarities	Differences
1.	1. 2. 3.	1. 2. 3.
2.	1. 2. 3.	1. 2. 3.

Type	Similarities	Differences
3.	1. 2. 3.	1. 2. 3.
4.	1. 2. 3.	1. 2. 3.
5.	1. 2. 3.	1. 2. 3.

3. Family Supports

In the space provided below, develop a web to display the many kinds of supports that families of students with autism may require. Include support from school, community agencies, extended family, etc., as well as the nature of the support (emotional, physical, financial).

VII. WEB ACTIVITIES

Everyday, more and more information is posted on the internet. This access to information allows for easier and in-depth study on issues and topics. Learning how to negotiate the internet develops a valuable skill which will assist you as you study and work with students with disabilities and their families. The weblinks for these activities, along with many other resources, can be found at the companion website for the text: www.ablongman.com/smith5e.

1. You have been approached by a parent who has a son that has been recently received a diagnosis of autism. She has asked for websites on autism that are specifically geared towards parents. See if you can find five sites that would be helpful for this mother. Here is one to get you started: www.autismfyi.org

2. You are a principle at an elementary school. The parents of an autistic child have approached you to inquire about enrolling their child in your school next year. Specifically, the parents want a curriculum for their child that will incorporate teaching methods reflective of applied behavior analysis. You explain to the parents that you do not know anything about ABA but you will do research on it and get back with them. Find some websites that will help you. Here's one to get you started: http://rsaffran.tripod.com/aba.html

VIII. FOCUS QUESTIONS

After studying the information presented in the textbook chapter and doing the exercises found in this study guide chapter, you should be able to answer the advance organizer questions listed at the beginning of the textbook chapter. Answer these questions to see if you need to review the material in this workbook and textbook again.

1. What is the relationship of autistic disorder, or autism, to autistic spectrum disorders?

2. What is meant by the term spectrum, and what does this term imply about people diagnosed with ASD?

3. What is the cause of autistic disorders? Why is this sometimes a controversial issue?

4. What are some ways in which the learning environment can be modified and adapted for students with autism?

5. Why should instruction in nonacademic areas such as social skills be included in educational programs for students with autism?

6. What are some of the implications or effects of autism being an "invisible" disability for the child and for the child's family? What are the implications for educators? For other professionals?

IX. THINKING ABOUT DILEMMAS TO SOLVE

Consider the following issues. Think broadly about how the dilemmas listed below might be solved in this new century. Remember, no "correct" answers or proven solutions to these problems have been agreed upon (or even tested). Regardless, they are important to students with disabilities and their families.

1. How do the three deficit areas (communication, social skills and range of interests) affect how and what children with autism learn?

2. How does the wide range of abilities within autism affect educational programming?

3. How do deficits in academic skills influence academic learning?

4. Name ways to educate the public about the facts of autism while debunking the myths of autism.

5. Discuss how autism affects the family.

6. What are instructional adaptations that educators can utilize for children with autism to allow for more inclusion in the general curriculum?

X. PUTTING IT ALL TOGETHER
Discussion questions:

a. How should debates about the definition of autism (such as restrictive vs. broad) be resolved? What is the impact of such decisions?

b. Explain possible reasons for the alarming and increasing prevalence of autism.

c. How can we ensure that funding for research and development of technology enhancements continue, and that people with disabilities have full access to new and emerging technologies?

d. In what ways will advances in instructional and assistive technologies continue to change the lives of people with severe disabilities, and how will events in classrooms have to adjust? How can policymakers insure schools will keep pace?

2. Mini-case Study:

In previous chapters, you were presented with mini-case studies. Using those as samples, create your own mini-case study for a child with one of the types of autistic spectrum disorders. Write the mini-case study, answer the questions, write some additional questions of your own, and answer them.

The Child's Case:

a. What special accommodations might the school need to make for this child?

b. In what special ways should the teacher work with this child's family?

c.

d.

e. Finish the story.

XI. PUZZLES: A TIME TO PLAY

Solve the puzzle below by rearranging the letters for each column. Remember, some words may wrap to the next line.

C		S	L			E	R			G		U					
F		I	E		S	H	N		E	D	D	R		E	S		
O	E	R	P	E	T	I	E	V	P	I	S	H	C	A	T	D	
W	H	I	E	R	C	E	A	T	E	E	O	T	I	D	E	R	O
N	T	H	N	D	R	C	A	L	W	A	T	U	N	A	S	I	O
								■					■				■
				■							■						■
					■											■	
	■								■								
	■			■				■					■	■	■	■	■

SOMETHING TO THINK ABOUT Changing the definition of autism affects its prevalence.

Across

1 Behavioral checklist used to identify autism (abbr.)

4 _____ deficits: Inability to mutually interact or to share interest in events or objects

8 Childhood Disintegrative Disorder

9 _____ syndrome: A little understood disability which shares many symptoms with autism.

11 Founder of the Autism Society of America

12 Type of autism; individual possesses unusual talents

15 autistic _____: A group of disorders or conditions which share some characteristics and behaviors originally described under the classification of autism

Down

1 Severe disorder of thinking, communication, interpersonal relationships, and behavior

2 Coined the term "autism"

3 _____ teaching: adapting materials and environment to help child make sense of world

5 Repeating exactly what was heard immediately or even days later.

6 People with autism often insist on this

7 Childhood Autism Rating Scale (abbr.)

10 Picture Exchange Communication System

13 Applied behavior analysis

14 According to IDEA, autistic characteristics are evident by this age

XII. MAKING CONNECTIONS

To imagine what life would be like with autism, read one family's story at
http://www.isn.net/~jypsy/
Answer the following questions:

1. What is your overall impression of their story?

2. Is Alex getting all the help he needs?

3. What is the family doing right?

4. What could the family be doing differently?

13

VERY LOW-INCIDENCE DISABILITIES: MULTIPLE-SEVERE DISABILITIES, DEAFBLINDNESS, TRAUMATIC BRAIN INJURY

I. IMPORTANT POINTS TO REMEMBER

> ➤ Multiple-severe disabilities, deaf-blindness and traumatic brain injury account for less than 1% of all schoolchildren.

> ➤ To be included in the deaf-blind category, students must meet these criterion: visual acuity of 20/70 or worse in the better eye and an auditory deficit of 30 dB in the better ear.

> ➤ TBI is often not immediately recognized or diagnosed.

> ➤ Low incidence disabilities are often severe, usually with multiple problems in cognition, language, speech or motor skills.

> ➤ Students with very low incidence disabilities are not included at a high rate in general education programs.

II. TIMELINE

Review the timeline presented below. Knowing something about the history of multiple-severe disabilities, no matter how short, may help you understand some of the issues related to students with these disabilities.

1904   Helen Keller graduates with honors from Radcliffe.

1990   Traumatic Brain Injury becomes a special education category when IDEA is reauthorized in 1990.

III. MAIN IDEAS AND DETAILS

Organize your notes efficiently by listing the *Main Ideas* in one column and relating at least two *Details* to each main idea. The table below was designed to help you organize your thoughts as you study this chapter in your textbook. To assist you, we provided either the *Main Ideas* or parts of the *Details*. Extra room has been provided to add additional topics for you to remember as you study.

Multiple-Severe Disabilities

Main Ideas	Details
1. Defined	1. 2. 3. 4.
2.	1. Only 0.18% students in this federal category 2.
3. Causes and prevention	1. 2.
4.	1. 2. 3. Difficulties with memory 4.

Deafblindness

Main Ideas	Details
5.	1. IDEA - 2. Baldwin -
6. Identification/prevalence	1. 2.
7.	1. 2. Hereditary causes 3. 4. National prevention programs
8. Characteristics	1. 2. 3. 4. 5.

Traumatic Brain Injury

9.	1. 2. Often has delayed diagnosis
10. Identification/impact	1. 2.
11. Causes and prevention	1. 2. accidents 3. 4.
12.	1. 2. uneven abilities 3. 4.

Very Low Incidence Disabilities

13. Educational Considerations	1. 2. 3. 4.
14.	1. 2. six steps in addressing concerns
15. Technology	1. 2. 3. 4.
16.	1. 2.
17.	1. 2.

IV. DEFINE THESE TERMS:

Define these important terms listed below. Remember, if you get stuck, you may use the glossary in the back of your textbook.

alternative portfolios

augmentive and alternative communication
devices

community based instruction

communication boards

deaf-blindness

distance education

family system

functional assessments

functionally behavior assessment

incidental learning

intervener

life skills

multiple-severe disabilities

positive behavioral supports

speech talkers

traumatic brain injury

Usher syndrome

V. ALPHABET SOUP

There are a number of abbreviations used in special education. Identify the following that relate to low incidence disabilities and were discussed in Chapter 13.

ACC

EDC

IDEA

IPE

TASH

TBI

 ## VI. STUDY ORGANIZERS

1. The Name Game

Person	Significant Accomplishments
Laura Dewey Bridgman	
Samuel Gidley Howe	

Rob Horner/ George Sugai	
Helen Keller	
Anne Sullivan	

2. Alternative portfolios

Some students with severe disabilities are being assessed via alternative portfolio. In the chart below, list the six areas that should be included in the portfolio and give examples for each area.

Area	Examples
1.	1. 2.
2.	1. 2.
3.	1. 2.

4.	1.
	2.
5.	1.
	2.
6.	1.
	2.

3. Family Supports

In the space provided below, develop a web to display the many kinds of supports that families of students with multiple-severe disabilities, TBI, or deaf-blindness may require. Include support from school, community agencies, extended family, etc., as well as the nature of the support (emotional, physical, financial).

VII. WEB ACTIVITIES

Everyday, more and more information is posted on the internet. This access to information allows for easier and in-depth study on issues and topics. Learning how to negotiate the internet develops a valuable skill which will assist you as you study and work with students with disabilities and their families. The weblinks for these activities, along with many other resources, can be found at the companion website for the text: www.ablongman.com/smith5e.

1. You have been appointed to a task force that will develop an advertising campaign to inform the public about how to prevent TBI. Develop a list of actions that prevent accidents, and suggest how children can be better protected. You might find some of these web sites helpful in your search: www.childrensdefense.org or www.909shot.com

2. Many people are unaware of the many different groups that promote sports, theater, and the arts for people with disabilities. See how many you can find and describe through the web. Here a few sites (Very Special Arts, Special Olympics, National Theater of the Deaf) to get you started: www.vsarts.org or www.specialolympics.org or www.ntd.org

VIII. FOCUS QUESTIONS

After studying the information presented in the textbook chapter and doing the exercises found in this study guide chapter, you should be able to answer the advance organizer questions listed at the beginning of the textbook chapter. Answer these questions to see if you need to review the material in this workbook and textbook again.

1. What are the major characteristics of children with severe-multiple disabilities?

2. How would you describe the impact of deaf-blindness on those affected?

3. How can many cases of TBI be prevented?

4. What are the key elements of functional behavioral assessments?

5. Why do many of these students receive their high school education in the community?

6. What comprises an appropriate education and the least restrictive environment for students with low incidence disabilities?

IX. THINKING ABOUT DILEMMAS TO SOLVE

Consider the following issues. Think broadly about how the dilemmas listed below might be solved in this new century. Remember, no "correct" answers or proven solutions to these problems have been agreed upon (or even tested). Regardless, they are important to students with disabilities and their families.

1. How should school officials determine whether the educational needs of students with low incidence disabilities are being met?

2. How can educators improve the chances of students with low incidence disabilities of achieving goals of independent living and full participation in the community?

3. Discuss the different kinds of support these students require during their school years and throughout life.

4. In what ways can the curriculum best provide these students with the skills they will need as adults?

5. What kind of technological supports might facilitate students with low incidence disabilities independence and full community presence as adults?

X. PUTTING IT ALL TOGETHER

1. Discussion questions:

a. Discuss ways educators can address the problem of isolation for students with deafblindness.

b. Should TBI be a separate special education category? What are functional reasons for this group of students being considered a distinctive group, rather than being included alongside students with learning disabilities or special health care needs?

c. How can we ensure that funding for research and development of technology enhancements continue, and that people with disabilities have full access to new and emerging technologies?

d. In what ways will advances in instructional and assistive technologies continue to change the lives of people with severe disabilities, and how will events in classrooms have to adjust? How can policymakers insure schools will keep pace?

2. Mini-case Study:

Tamara's story: Toward the end of the summer before fifth grade, Tamara did what her mother had always told her not to do: she took a ride on her brother's friend's motorcycle. She was riding behind him when they crashed. Tamara hit her head on the pavement, but didn't cut herself. She went home and took a nap. She didn't want to tell her mother, but after several days of headaches, she did. He mother took her to the doctor, who said that she'd be fine.

   a. Tamara's new fifth grade teacher noticed that Tamara was distractible. She had trouble focusing on her studies, seemed to get tired easily, and was not keeping up with her classmates. She mentioned this to Tamara's old fourth grade teacher, who expressed surprise for Tamara had always been one of her best students. What should Tamara's fifth grade teacher do next?

   b. What should happen at the parent conference the teacher held with Tamara's mother?

   c. What accommodations should the school make for Tamara?

   d. Finish the story.

XI. PUZZLES: A TIME TO PLAY

Across

3 Organizing and arranging environments so problem behaviors are less likely to occur

6 Traumatic Brain Injury

7 Group most at risk for TBI

8 _____ learning: type of learning where knowledge is gained

9 Works one-on-one with a deafblind student

10 Teacher of Helen Keller

12 Can prevent many cases of TBI if used

13 _____ portfolios: Schoolwork becomes documentation of progress at school

Down

1 Often occurs with TBI

2 _____ education: Instruction delivered via technology

4 Technology that speaks for an individual

5 Famous person with deafblindness

11 A syndrome which causes blindness

Solve the puzzle below by rearranging the letters for each column. Remember, some words may wrap to the next line.

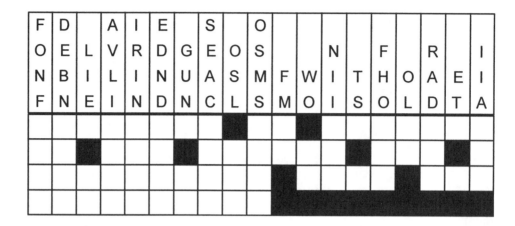

XII. MAKING CONNECTIONS

Go to http://www.aidb.org/aidb/helenkeller.asp and read this synopsis of Helen Keller's life and answer the following questions:

1. Despite such a severity of disability, her life was more successful than some who do not have disabilities. What factors contributed to her success?

2. In what ways would her life be different if she had been born in 21st century?

3. Do you think she would have still been famous had she been born in the 21st century? Why or why not?

4. Would it be easier to acquire deafblindness at birth or later in life? Explain your rationale.

CHAPTER TESTS

CHAPTER 1

1.1   The concept of disability

    a. is always synonymous with that of a handicap.
    b. varies by culture.
    c. did not develop until the last century, and so is relatively new.
    d. refers primarily to individuals with physical disabilities.

1.2   Which professional founded an organization that later became the AAMR?

    a. Maria Montessori
    b. Thomas Hopkins Gallaudet
    c. Helen Keller
    d. Edouard Seguin

1.3   Which court case ended "separate but equal" schools and was used to fight the exclusion of children with disabilities from public schools?

    a. *PARC v. Commonwealth of Pennsylvania*
    b. *Brown v. Board of Education*
    c. *Mills v. Board of Education of the District of Columbia*
    d. *Honig v. Doe*

1.4   Which of the following provides adults with disabilities greater access to employment and participation in everyday activities by barring discrimination in employment, transportation, public accommodations, and telecommunications?

    a. PL 94-142
    b. IDEA
    c. IDEA '97
    d. The Americans with Disabilities Act

1.5 Section 504 and the ADA are considered to be

    a. civil rights laws.
    b. discriminatory laws.
    c. outdated.
    d. responsible for increased negative attitudes and subsequent discrimination toward people with disabilities.

1.6 Which is the largest special education professional organization in the United States?

    a. American Association on Mental Retardation
    b. Learning Disabilities Association
    c. Association for Individuals with ADHD
    d. Council for Exceptional Children

1.7 Which of the following is a good example of a normalization activity?

    a. riding the same school bus as the other children
    b. working
    c. taking risks
    d. all of the above

1.8 Which one of the following is NOT a defining feature of special education, according to IDEA?

    a. FAPE
    b. LRE
    c. individually-determined educational program
    d. inclusion in general education programs at all times

1.9 IDEA identifies _____ disability categories.

    a. 3
    b. 10
    c. 13
    d. 18

1.10 Which of the following reflects the proper terminology to refer to someone with a disability?

    a. the mentally retarded
    b. a mentally retarded child
    c. a child with mental retardation
    d. the disabled

Short Answers:

1.11 Explain the similarities and differences between the ADA and IDEA.

1.12 Why has litigation played such an important role in special education?

1.13 What is special education?

1.14 Explain the differences between having a disability and being handicapped.

1.15   How is the concept of normalization related to LRE?

Application:

1.16   Imagine the field of special education fifty years into the future. Do you think that legislation and litigation will still have the impact on the field that they do today? Why or why not?

CHAPTER 2

2.1   What is the major complaint of special education teachers regarding IEPs?

   a. They are too confusing and complicated.
   b. They should be written by administrators.
   c. They contribute to a burden of too much paperwork.
   d. They are not sufficient to ensure student progress.

2.2   Which student is NOT eligible for special education services under IDEA?

   a. Jacob, an infant with Down syndrome.
   b. Jorge, a third-grader with autism.
   c. Jennifer, a college student with a learning disability.
   d. Joseph, a 14-year-old with a behavioral disorder who lives in a juvenile correction facility.

2.3   A special office or function that assists in the referral process is

   a. the children's placement service.
   b. The Child at Risk.
   c. Child Find.
   d. child referral.

2.4   Which acronym refers to the need for children with disabilities to interact with their nondisabled peers as much as possible?

   a. ERA
   b. FAPE
   c. CCD
   d. LRE

2.5   Ms. Battle, a speech-language pathologist, travels to five different elementary schools in one district, working with children and teachers at each school. This is an example of

    a. full inclusion.
    b. collaborative teaching.
    c. a center school program.
    d. an itinerant service.

2.6   If Carlos's IEP team determines that he should be placed in a resource room to receive instruction in math,

    a. he must be removed from the general education classroom whenever any type of math instruction occurs.
    b. they are in violation of IDEA.
    c. they have violated the tenets of LRE.
    d. his IEP must delineate why he cannot participate in general education for that portion of the day.

2.7   An evaluation battery of tests includes

    a. intelligence tests.
    b. academic achievement tests.
    c. acuity tests.
    d. all of the above.

2.8   An IFSP is evaluated

    a. annually.
    b. every six months with the family.
    c. every month with a specialist.
    d. a and b.

2.9   One important principle when developing IEPs is that

    a. services which are unavailable may be left off the IEP.
    b. all services listed do not necessarily have to be provided.
    c. all of the student's needs must be met.
    d. all of the above.

2.10 Unlike most IFSPs and IEPs, _____ should be a full participating member of the multidisciplinary team when discussing transition issues.

   a. a parent
   b. the special education teacher
   c. the general education teacher
   d. the student

Short answers:

2.11 List the types of special education placements available to students with disabilities, and discuss whether different educational environments are necessary. Please explain your answer.

2.12 Discuss the roles of the various professionals that may be involved in the service delivery process.

2.13 Compare and explain the differences in these terms: array, cascade, and continuum.

2.14 Discuss the purposes of the transition component to IEPs, and describe what should be included.

2.15 Discuss the differences between IFSPs and IEPs.

Application:

2.16   Miguel is a 16-year-old student with mental retardation. Miguel has a possible job as a bus boy in a restaurant, but he needs to learn how to set and clear a table. Write the behavioral goals and objectives for this skill.

CHAPTER 3

3.1 Which risk factor associated with poverty places culturally and linguistically diverse students at greater risk for being identified as having a disability?

   a. lack of access to health care
   b. exposure to environmental toxins
   c. attending poor schools
   d. all of the above

3.2 Gary complains to his parents that his teacher talks too much, makes him maintain eyecontact with her, and asks questions that are inappropriately personal. These concerns are consistent with students who are

   a. Native American.
   b. European American.
   c. gifted but have learning disabilities.
   d. low-achievers.

3.3 How can discrimination in the assessment process occur?

   a. the content of test items relates only to one culture's experiences
   b. diverse populations are not represented in the standardization population
   c. the evaluator is untrained in multicultural or bilingual techniques
   d. all of the above

3.4 Which court case questioned possible bias in intelligence tests resulting in a large number of Hispanic children classified as having mental retardation?

   a. *Parents in Action on Special Education (PASE) v. Hannon*
   b. *Larry P. v. Riles*
   c. *Diana v. State Board of Education*
   d. *Lau v. Nichols*

3.5   Which racial or ethnic group is frequently overrepresented in special education classes?

    a. African American
    b. Native American
    c. Hispanic
    d. all of the above

3.6   Researchers have found that the most common disability among students who are homeless is/are

    a. learning disabilities.
    b. mental retardation.
    c. blindness.
    d. emotional or behavioral disorders.

3.7   A Native American child is referred for behavioral assessment because she/he refuses to compete in gym class. This may demonstrate

    a. a correct referral.
    b. a conflict between peers and the child's culture.
    c. cross-cultural dissonance.
    d. none of the above.

3.8   When Mira first moved to the United States from India last year, she received instruction in her native language, Bengali. She now receives instruction in both languages. What type of approach are her teachers using?

    a. total immersion
    b. ESL
    c. sheltered instruction
    d. bilingual education

3.9   Approximately how many years does it take to acquire complex language abilities required for academic work?

   a. two-three
   b. three-five
   c. five-seven
   d. seven-eight

3.10   _____ partnerships are often overlooked by educators who work with students from diverse backgrounds.

   a. Teacher-principal
   b. Elementary-middle school
   c. School-community
   d. None of the above

Short answers:

3.11   Why do some professionals believe there is a misrepresentation of culturally and linguistically diverse students in some special education categories (consider both overrepresentation and underrepresentation)?

3.12   Describe the unique needs of students who are homeless and ways that educators can address these needs.

3.13   Explain how culture can affect a family's views regarding disabilities.

3.14   How are the effects of poverty and culture often confused?

3.15   Explain the differences between cultural diversity and linguistic diversity.

3.16   You are a teacher in a rural and geographically isolated area. Several of your students are Hispanic and the language used in the home is Spanish. Develop a plan to work closely with these students' families.

Chapter 4

4.1   Nine-year-old Shania expects failure and sees little use in expending any effort to learn. Shania's behavior is characteristic of

    a. students who are resistant to treatment.
    b. students with an internal locus of control.
    c. a low achiever.
    d. ADHD.

4.2   _____ is a newly emerging and defining characteristic of learning disabilities where students do not respond to validated methods typically applied in general education settings and require intensive, individualized instruction.

    a. Resistant to treatment
    b. ADHD
    c. Impulsivity
    d. Low achievement

4.3   _____ is/are used to determine the difference between a child's actual achievement and expected achievement based on the student's IQ scores.

    a. IQ tests
    b. Standardized achievement tests
    c. Discrepancy formulas
    d. High stakes assessment

4.4   The process/product debate was finally resolved when research analysis by Hammill and Larsen showed that _____ approaches were seldom effective in teaching academic skills.

    a. modality-centered
    b. physical exericse
    c. perceptual approaches
    d. direct instruction

4.5   Out of 100 schoolchildren, about how many will be identified as having a learning disability?

   a. two
   b. five
   c. six
   d. ten

4.6   Early instruction on sound-symbol awareness during the preschool years

   a. may reduce the degree of a reading disability that would have become apparent during the school years.
   b. can completely prevent learning disabilities.
   c. can confuse a child and increase the chances of developing a learning disability.
   d. has been linked to improved social skills and stronger problem-solving abilities among at-risk children.

4.7   _____ is the inner drive that causes individuals to be energized and directed in their behavior.

   a. Learned helplessness
   b. External locus of control
   c. Attribution
   d. Motivation

4.8   Before starting each lesson, Mr. Ndabge asks his students a few questions to get them thinking about the information he is about to present. This is an example of

   a. generalization
   b. an organizing routine.
   c. CBM.
   d. behavior modification.

4.9　ShaQuita is a first-year teacher working with students with learning disabilities. When selecting instructional techniques, she should be sure to

    a.　choose those that are interesting or fun for her to administer.
    b.　use the latest methods discussed by fellow teachers.
    c.　choose techniques that are verified through rigorous research.
    d.　ask the children what techniques they like the best.

4.10　Adults with learning disabilities

    a.　are often underemployed.
    b.　typically have at least an undergraduate degree, and often a graduate degree.
    c.　are usually completely independent and are able to support themselves.
    d.　have the lowest employment rates of any of the disability categories.

Short answer:

4.11　List the key components of the federal government's definition of learning disabilities.

4.12　Discuss the criticisms of discrepancy formulas.

4.13　Discuss the results of the MacMillan, Gresham, and Bocian (1998) study and the implications for the identification of students with learning disabilities.

4.14   Although learning disabilities is primarily related to academic difficulties, many of these youngsters present behavioral problems to their parents and teachers. Why do you think this is the case?

4.15   Discuss four factors that contribute to successful parent-teacher conferences.

Application:

4.16   Imagine that you have a learning disability. What strategies would you use to be successful in your college courses?

CHAPTER 5

5.1   The letters of the alphabet are examples of

    a. written symbols.
    b. vocal symbols.
    c. sign language.
    d. verbal communication.

5.2   _____ result in an abnormal spoken language production, characterized by an unusual pitch, loudness, or quality of sounds.

    a. Dysfluencies
    b. Voice problems
    c. Fluency problems
    d. Articulation problems

5.3   A toddler who says, "Yook Mommy, yook!" rather than "Look Mommy, look!" is displaying what type of articulation error?

    a. omission.
    b. substitution.
    c. distortion.
    d. addition.

5.4   _____ was/were one of the first to develop screening procedures to identify persons with speech problems and hearing losses, and began clinical and research programs.

    a. ASHA.
    b. Public schools
    c. The military
    d. The U.S. Department of Education

5.5   Micah has an opening in the roof of his mouth that allows excessive air and sound waves to flow through the nasal cavities, resulting in a very nasal-sounding voice and difficulty producing some sounds. Micah has

a. a language disorder.
b. a cleft palate.
c. a language delay.
d. problems with fluency and pitch.

5.6   Which of the following is characteristic of a child with a language impairment?

a. exhibits dysfluencies
b. is unable to follow oral directions
c. has poor voice quality
d. makes consistent and age-inappropriate articulation errors

5.7   Which of the following is NOT a factor that teachers should consider when concerned about a child's speech or language abilities?

a. age
b. setting
c. popularity
d. stress

5.8   Ms. Allinder, an early childhood educator, wants to conduct an activity where she can lead opportunities for language development, vocabulary building, phonemic awareness, and social exchanges. She should

a. play music and encourage the students to dance.
b. let the students play outside.
c. have each child choose an independent play activity.
d. read a story with her class.

5.9   Which of the following instructional enhancements would you use to help a student learn the sequence of events leading up to the Boston Tea Party?

    a.   attribute web
    b.   script or story framework
    c.   Venn diagram
    d.   multiple-meaning tree

5.10   Which strategy should Ms. Gaff use to help her students learn the meanings of content words in her biology class?

    a.   script and story framework
    b.   Venn diagram
    c.   multiple-meaning tree
    d.   role-playing

Short Answer:

5.11   Describe the 3 types of speech impairments, and the kinds of problems common within each one.

5.12   Distinguish between language impairments, language delays, and language differences.

5.13   How can teachers promote the language development of preschool children?

5.14   How would you modify your classroom instructional techniques to ensure success for students with speech or language impairments?

5.15   Describe the different types of technology used by people with speech or language impairments.

Application:

5.16   You are a regular educator attending an IEP meeting where the decision about the educational placement and the educational program of a student with a severe articulation problem is being discussed. What suggestions would you make for this student?

CHAPTER 6

6.1 Pearl has an IQ of 42 and requires a limited level of support to live independently and work in a cafeteria. Under which level of severity would she be classified?

    a. mild mental retardation
    b. moderate mental retardation
    c. severe mental retardation
    d. profound mental retardation

6.2 Which of the following would NOT be considered a conceptual adaptive skill?

    a. getting dressed
    b. making change
    c. figuring out what to do if you miss the bus to work
    d. reading

6.3 Peter is a young adult with mental retardation. Although Peter's parents are worried that he will take the wrong city bus to his new job, they have decided to give in to his repeated requests for independence and stop driving him to work. Their decision is in concert with the concept of

    a. self-advocacy
    b. dignity of risk.
    c. deinstitutionalization.
    d. systems of support.

6.4 Most students with mental retardation fall within the _____ range.

    a. mild
    b. moderate
    c. severe
    d. profound

6.5   When Renaldo was born, doctors discovered that most of his brain was missing. Renaldo has

     a. spina bifida.
     b. anencephaly.
     c. asphyxia.
     d. hydrocephaly.

6.6   The two major sources of lead and subsequent lead poisoning

     a. continue to be produced in the United States.
     b. are no longer a threat to children in this country.
     c. are exhaust fumes from leaded gasoline and lead-based paint.
     d. are not causes of mental retardation.

6.7   Danielle, an adult with mental retardation, bags groceries in the checkout line in the local supermarket. Her co-workers provide helpful reminders to her such as, "Don't put the bread in the bottom of the bag." This is an example of a _____ support.

     a. nonpaid
     b. generic
     c. natural
     d. specialized

6.8   Which of the following is NOT a key feature of effective inclusive preschools?

     a. about a third of the students have disabilities
     b. half-day program
     c. accredited
     d. family partnerships

6.9   Which factor has been shown to make a clear difference in the life satisfaction of individuals in community living settings.

     a. the number of people living in the setting
     b. the salary that the individual makes
     c. the amount of free time available
     d. the ability to make choices

6.10   Many students with disabilities are now able to include e-mail as part of their school and daily life through a program called

    a. Miles for Mail.
    b. the Arc.
    c. Best Buddies.
    d. e-Buddies

Short Answer:

6.11   Explain why IQ tests are still used for identification purposes, and what alternatives are being considered.

6.12   Describe characteristics and long-term outcomes for children with fetal alcohol syndrome.

6.13   Explain the 4 sources of supports available to people with mental retardation, and give an example of each.

6.14   Provide 5 examples of what a functional curriculum in mathematics would contain.

6.15 Develop a task analysis for doing laundry. Test your task analysis the next time you do your own laundry. Did you leave any steps out?

Application:

6.16 You are a teacher of high school students with mental retardation and need to prepare an instructional unit on how to conduct weekly grocery shopping. To plan and provide a framework for your lessons, conduct a task analysis of this activity.

CHAPTER 7

7.1   A child who loves to build with any available materials-Lincoln logs, blocks, straws, toothpicks- demonstrates which of Gardner's intelligences.

    a. linguistic
    b. spatial
    c. intrapersonal
    d. naturalist

7.2   As a result of Sputnik, federal funding was appropriated to

    a. establish programs for gifted education.
    b. develop ways to identify students with high academic achievement.
    c. conduct research to find effective methods for providing excellent educational   experiences.
    d. all of the above.

7.3   Smart School District has decided to use a more inclusive approach to identifying students, and so will not use an IQ score as a sole means of identification. The superintendent wants to know how many students to budget gifted education for. Based on information in your text, how many would you recommend?

    a. less than 3%
    b. 3% to 5%
    c. 5% to 10%
    d. 10% to 15%

7.4   Which of the following is NOT a common social/emotional characteristic of gifted children?

    a. criticizes self
    b. is nonconforming
    c. does not take risks
    d. is intense

7.5   Roderick is a gifted student, but is unidentified because his underachievement, disorganization, distractibility and impulsivity mask his giftedness. Roderick's behavior is characteristic of children who are gifted and

    a. have ADHD.
    b. have Asperger's syndrome.
    c. are culturally diverse.
    d. have a hearing loss.

7.6   Jeff attends a regular history class, but uses self-directed learning to study topics in more depth and work on problems in which he has a particular interest. This is an example of

    a. independent study.
    b. a mentorship.
    c. an internship.
    d. the revolving door model.

7.7   Star High School has 12 sophomores who all have advanced skills in algebra and trigonometry. The school places them all in the senior-level calculus class. This is an example of

    a. curriculum compacting.
    b. ability grouping.
    c. cluster grouping.
    d. an internship.

7.8   A teaching technique that involves studying various positions on an issue in an attempt to learn more about a topic refers to

    a. internships.
    b. independent study.
    c. interdisciplinary instruction.
    d. the Revolving Door Model.

7.9   Natalie attends a special high school for the performing arts. She had to audition in order to be accepted. Natalie attends a(n)

    a. pull-out program.

   b. magnet school.
   c. accelerated program.
   d. community college.

7.10 Many gifted students appear to be more mature than others their age,

   a. which can be deceptive and result in stress for the child.
   b. which can be helpful for parents who are preparing their children for the transition to adult life.
   c. a fact that parents should remember and thus treat them as if they were 2-3 years older than their actual age.
   d. a frustrating characteristic listed by many parents who have difficulty disciplining their gifted children.

Short Answer:

7.11 Explain how creativity is not fostered, and in may cases discouraged, in American schools and society.

7.12 List some explanations for the underrepresentation of students from diverse backgrounds in gifted education programs, and discuss what needs to happen to change this situation.

7.13 Discuss the growth in special classes and schools for gifted students. Describe these programs.

7.14 Describe some accommodations for twice-exceptional students that you could implement in your own classroom.

7.15   Discuss how long-term outcomes for gifted and talented students can be improved.

Application:

7.16   You have been hired by a Native American tribe to develop procedures to identify students who are gifted and should receive specialized educational services. Describe the process you will use and the procedures you will propose.

CHAPTER 8

8.1 Which of the following is NOT one of the characteristics of emotional disturbance described in IDEA?

a. a short-term mood of unhappiness or depression
b. an inability to learn that cannot be explained by intellectual, sensory, or health factors
c. inappropriate types of behavior under normal circumstances
d. an inability to build or maintain satisfactory interpersonal relationships with peers and teachers.

8.2 In which case would a child probably NOT be described as hyperactive?

a. when the activity the child engages in is admired
b. when the child fidgets and squirms in his seat during class
c. when a child is unable to stay seated when expected to do so
d. an inability to play in quiet leisure activities with friends

8.3 All of the following are internalizing behaviors EXCEPT for

a. anorexia
b. bulimia
c. depression
d. defiance

8.4 Students who have ADHD and antisocial behavior are often ineligible for special services because

a. they are usually living in juvenile correctional facilities.
b. they drop out of school before an evaluation can occur.
c. their parents refuse placement.
d. violent behavioral events do not occur at a high rate.

8.5   Which person wrote the book Child Psychiatry, that stimulated the development of services for children in America?

a. Leo Kanner
b. Samuel Gridley Howe
c. William Healy
d. Augusta Bronner

8.6   The three general areas which can contribute to emotional or behavioral disorders are

a. biology, home and community, and school.
b. biology, prenatal factors, home.
c. prenatal factors, home and community, and school.
d. substance abuse, parental neglect, and income level.

8.7   More than any other group of children with disabilities, students with emotional or behavioral disorders present problems with

a. internalizing behaviors.
b. social skills.
c. academic deficits.
d. sleep disorders.

8.8   Students are less likely to engage in disruptive behaviors when

a. they are engaged in academic work.
b. the teacher maintains an authoritarian model of discipline.
c. they exhibit externalizing behaviors.
d. the teacher is really nice to them.

8.9   Which conceptual model uses physiological interventions such as medications and biofeedback?

a. biogenic approach
b. humanistic approach
c. ecological approach
d. behavioral approach

8.10   Points, privileges, and praise are all examples of

   a. behavior specific praise.
   b. positive reinforcement.
   c. group contingencies.
   d. negative consequences.

Short Answer:

8.11   Describe the characteristics of schizophrenia and Tourette's syndrome.

8.12   Discuss evaluation procedures that have been recommended to prevent the disproportionate number of African American males identified as having emotional or behavioral disorders.

8.13   Explain what you can do within your own classroom to help prevent the development of emotional or behavioral disorders in your students.

8.14   How do peers perceive students with emotional or behavioral disorders? What could you do in your class to facilitate peer acceptance of these students?

8.14   A child in your class displays aggressive behavior towards his classmates. Select one of the conceptual models from Table 8.3 and develop an intervention plan based upon that model. Describe what you would do.

Application:

8.16   Set up your own "Point-Counterpoint" debate about applying the principles of full inclusion to the education of students with emotional and behavioral disorders.

Chapter 9

9.1   According to the federal definition for other health impairments, the health problem

   a. must be chronic or acute.
   b. does not necessarily have to affect the child's educational performance.
   c. must have developed before the age of 18.
   d. needs to be verified by two independent medical personnel.

9.2   Moniqueka has a spinal cord disorder that limits her muscular control and movement. She has a(n)

   a. neuromotor impairment.
   b. muscular/skeletal condition.
   c. chronic illness.
   d. infectious disease.

9.3   Melvin has juvenile arthritis, a condition that affects his joints and limits his functioning. Melvin has a

   a. neuromotor impairment.
   b. muscular/skeletal condition.
   c. chronic illness.
   d. infectious disease.

9.4   Jason has periods during which he appears to be clowning around, but is in fact exhibiting automatic behavior resulting from seizures. Jason is having _____ seizures.

   a. absence or petit mal
   b. simple partial
   c. complex partial
   d. generalized tonic-clonic

9.5   Which of the following is appropriate treatment for a generalized tonic-clonic seizure?

    a. give liquids immediately after seizure
    b. restrain the individual to avoid injury
    c. place a spoon in the individual's mouth to prevent tongue-biting
    d. turn on side to keep airway clear

9.6   Ashley has cerebral palsy. Impairments in balance and depth make movements such as walking quite difficult. Which type of cerebral palsy does she have?

    a. spastic
    b. athetoid
    c. ataxia
    d. quadriplegia

9.7   For students with sickle cell anemia, there seems to be a correlation between the sickling crisis and

    a. emotional stress.
    b. strenuous exercise.
    c. consistency of diet.
    d. both a and b.

9.8   Carmen has spastic cerebral palsy, and sitting in typical classroom chairs is difficult for her. Which professional would design and build a special seating system for her?

    a. rehabilitation engineer
    b. occupational therapist
    c. physical therapist
    d. school nurse

9.9   Your text discussed three constant themes in the prevention of physical impairments and special health care needs. Which one of the following was NOT one of those themes?

  a. good prenatal care
  b. universal immunization programs
  c. gene therapy
  d. avoidance of injuries

9.10   Which of the following is NOT something that a service animal can do?

  a. use car keys to start a car engine
  b. dial a speakerphone
  c. pass out papers in class
  d. get food from the refrigerator

Short Answer:

9.11   Describe how teachers can work with students with ADHD to improve their educational and social outcomes.

9.12   In 1997, IDEA allowed for some children with ADHD to be included in the health impairments category. Explain why the federal government thought that only a small number of additional students would be eligible for special education, and whether their prediction was accurate.

9.13   What precautions and preventive techniques can teachers use in the classroom to fight infectious diseases?

9.14 There are specific communication issues that teachers of young children with physical disabilites should be aware of. Discuss them.

9.15 List some of the medical management duties that teachers are now being asked to perform, and discuss important considerations for teachers.

Application:

9.16 You are a general education teacher who has been informed by your school's principal that a new student will be joining your classroom. This child has cerebral palsy with diplegia. To prepare for this student, indicate the accommodations you will make to the physical arrangement of your classroom.

Chapter 10

10.1   With her hearing aid on, Rosa is able to comprehend others' speech and oral communication. Rosa is

a. deaf.
b. hard of hearing.
c. not really deaf.
d. just a little.

10.2   Dennis lost his hearing as a teenager. He is

a. profoundly deaf.
b. prelingually deaf.
c. postlingually deaf.
d. hard of hearing.

10.3   The _____ and the _____ make up the inner ear.

a. pinna; auditory canal
b. ossicles; eardrum
c. semicircular canals; cochlea
d. ossicles; Eustachian tube

10.4   Mr. and Mrs. Ndabge want to have their newborn's hearing tested. Which test will probably be used?

a. an air-conduction audiometry assessment
b. the otoacoustic emissions test
c. the bone-conduction method
d. the Snellen chart

10.5 All of the children below have the same level of hearing loss. Which child will experience the LEAST amount of cognitive or linguistic delays?

    a. Martinique, identified at 4 months
    b. Mabel, identified at 8 months
    c. Muriel, identified at 18 months
    d. Maecie, identified at 24 months

10.6 Educators have found that deaf college students tend to

    a. focus more on the words they are reading than on the meaning of the text.
    b. have much higher reading comprehension skills than college students without hearing   losses.
    c. only skim the content of the material in their textbooks, relying on Web-based information to gain information on their studies.
    d. all of the above.

10.7 The positive reading and language outcomes for deaf children of deaf parents occur to a large part because

    a. they learn oral language first.
    b. they are identified at a later age.
    c. they attend center schools.
    d. they learn language during the proper developmental period.

10.8 Ms. Schery wants to use ASL to teach English as a second language to her deaf students. She should use which approach?

    a. ASL
    b. total communication approach
    c. bilingual-bicultural approach
    d. oral-only approach

10.9   An employer wants to be sure that she complies with the Americans with Disabilities Act regarding one of her employees who is deaf. She should know that

   a. accommodations are determined on an individual basis.
   b. an interpreter is not considered to be an accommodation.
   c. the only accommodations she needs to make are purchase special phones and phone lines.
   d. all of the above.

10.10   To Deaf parents, the birth of a Deaf child is typically

   a. a source of embarrassment.
   b. a great celebration and a great relief.
   c. a cause for great worry.
   d. anticipated as completely normal.

Short Answer:

10.11   Explain how the process of hearing works.

10.12   What is meant by "Deaf culture?" Why is it so important to many adults who are deaf?

10.13   Discuss the factors that influence how well cochlear implants work.

10.14   Explain what you would do in your own classroom to ensure a positive working relationship with an interpreter.

10.15 List three types of assistive devices and give examples of each.

Application:

10.16 You are a general education teacher who has a hard-of-hearing child in your class. What accommodations would you make for this child? What special activities might you include in your instructional program to enhance this child's social integration?

CHAPTER 11

11.1 The _____ expands and contracts in response to the intensity of light that it receives.

    a. iris
    b. lens
    c. retina
    d. cornea

11.2 Tara holds her hands at arm's length in front of her face, and gradually moves them to the side until she can no longer see them. She is probably testing her

    a. visual depth.
    b. visual efficiency.
    c. visual acuity.
    d. peripheral vision.

11.3 Severe limitation in peripheral vision is sometimes called

    a. visual efficiency.
    b. tunnel vision.
    c. visual acuity.
    d. central vision.

11.4 Northeast School District has 10,000 students in its public schools. Based on national data, about how many of them would you anticipate to have low vision or blindness?

    a. 4
    b. 10
    c. 40
    d. 14

11.5   The system for reading and writing that Louis Braille developed was

a. very different from the braille system used today.
b. based upon a ten-point system, with three different heights of dots.
c. actually a raised version of the actual printed letters.
d. an embossed six-dot cell system.

11.6   Blind and low vision children are usually _____ in the development of play skills.

a. delayed about 2 years behind their sighted peers
b. delayed about 4 years behind their sighted peers
c. equivalent to their sighed peers
d. advanced when compared to their sighted peers

11.7   Orientation and mobility training should begin _____, with introduction of the long cane occurring between ages _____.

a. around age 2; 6 and 8.
b. around age 4; 10 and 12.
c. as soon as possible; 2 and 6.
d. at birth; 14 and 16.

11.8   Ms. McKinnon has a student with a visual disability in her class who requires a lot of bulky equipment and aids. Because of this, Ms. McKinnon will probably have to modify

a. the classroom's physical space.
b. the classroom rules.
c. the way she gives directions.
d. the amount of background noise in the class.

11.9   Students with low vision and blindness have one of the _____ high school graduation rates of all students with disabilities, and one of the _____ rates of competitive employment.

a. highest; highest
b. highest; lowest
c. lowest; highest
d. lowest; lowest

11.10   As part of understanding of their own visual differences, children need to gain knowledge about

a.   their visual status.
b.   the cause of their vision problem.
c.   the probability of their vision problem worsening or improving.
d.   all of the above.

Short Answer:

11.11   Discuss the impact of medical advances on both causes and prevention of visual disabilities.

11.12   List some ways that teachers can facilitate the development of communication and interaction skills among preschoolers with visual disabilities.

11.13   Explain how general education teachers can make accommodations for students with visual disabilities in their classrooms.

11.14   Describe some of the ways in which blind and low vision individuals now have greater access to the community.

11.15   Discuss the many target skills that parents address with children with severe visual disabilities.

Application:

11.16   You are a special educator attending an IEP meeting where the decision about the educational placement of a blind student is being discussed. To assist the parents in making a decision, list benefits of blind students attending their neighborhood schools and the benefits of their attending the state residential center school.

CHAPTER 12

12.1   Brittany has autism and mental retardation. She

    a. has low-functioning autism.
    b. has high-functioning autism.
    c. has Asperger's syndrome.
    d. is an autistic sauvant.

12.2   Which of the following is NOT a possible explanation for the increase in children identified as having autism?

    a. overidentification of children from culturally and linguistically diverse backgrounds due to language differences
    b. improved diagnostic methods
    c. use of the broader term ASD rather than the narrower term autism
    d. an actual increase in the condition

12.3   Which of the following has been proven to cause autism in children?

    a. environmental toxins
    b. cold interactional style of the child's mother
    c. childhood vaccines
    d. none of the above

12.4   Which characteristic is typical of a child with autism?

    a. marked distress over trivial or minor environmental changes
    b. ritualized daily routines
    c. obsessive and compulsive behaviors
    d. all of the above

12.5 As a teacher, which of the following skills should you teach directly to a young child with autism?

a. how to play with toys
b. how to play alone
c. verbal imitation, similar to echolalia
d. all of the above

12.6 Individuals with autism are often unable to keep jobs because

a. they do not develop strong job skills.
b. they are unable to learn.
c. they never learn to speak or to read.
d. of their social performance.

12.7 Which of the following is NOT part of the ABC model of data collection?

a. Antecedents
b. Analysis
c. Behavior
d. Consequences

12.8 Using concrete examples, providing feedback about the appropriateness of responses, and telling a child when behavior is proper are examples of how teachers of children with autism

a. communicate instructions and consequences carefully.
b. make events predictable.
c. foster positive participation.
d. teach using incidental learning.

12.9 Which of the following outcomes would indicate that an adult with autism participates socially by interacting with his co-workers?

a. The person with autism interacts with co-workers at social occasions that occur outside of work.
b. Co-workers advocate for or support the person.
c. The person with autism indicates increased self-esteem.
d. The person with autism is able to interpret and discriminate social cues.

12.10 The last phase that students engage in when using PECS is

  a. initiating communications.
  b. introducing sentence structure.
  c. choosing the message within PECS.
  d. expanding the use of pictures.

Short Answer:

12.11 Compare and contrast the National Research Council, IDEA, and the DSM-IV definitions of ASD.

12.12 Explain some of the professional suggestions for organizing the types of disabilities within the ASD umbrella.

12.13 Describe how a teacher would help a child with autism to develop functionally equivalent behaviors.

12.14 How can a general education teacher create an inclusive classroom where children with autism can participate successfully?

12.15 Explain how the Picture Exchange communication System works.

Application:

12.16 You are a special education teacher who is preparing an autistic child to join a general education class for music, art, and PE every week. What are the setting demands that the child must be aware of? What accommodations need to be made for this child? How would you interact with the general education teacher and students to prepare them for this situation? In what ways can you plan for success with this program?

CHAPTER 13

13.1   Modern definitions of disabilities describe individuals with multiple disabilities by

  a. what they can accomplish with a system of supports.
  b. what they can accomplish independently.
  c. deficits - what they cannot do.
  d. using a medical orientation.

13.2   Which of the following is NOT one of the areas of support listed in the TASH definition of severe disabilities?

  a. community living.
  b. employment.
  c. family planning.
  d. self-sufficiency.

13.3   Mr. Houston wants to assess the skills of a student with multiple-severe disabilities. Which of the following should he use?

  a. an array of traditional standardized tests
  b. functional assessments
  c. an IQ test
  d. tests of basic academic skill areas

13.4   The majority of individuals with deafblindness

  a. are academically gifted.
  b. rely on cued speech for communication purposes.
  c. function within normal academic levels.
  d. have other disabilities like mental retardation.

13.5 According to IDEA, an individual with deafblindness

    a. must have concomitant hearing and visual impairments ranging in severity from mild to severe.
    b. cannot have additional cognitive disabilities.
    c. who also has severe communication needs would be considered eligible under the speech or language impairments category rather than deafblindness.
    d. cannot be educated in special education programs without supplementary assistance to   address their unique educational needs.

13.6 A student with visual acuity of 20/70 in his better eye and an auditory deficit of 30 dB in his better ear

    a. qualifies as having deafblindness in most states.
    b. qualifies as having deafblindness in only a few states.
    c. falls within the universal criterion for deafblindness.
    d. does not qualify as having deafblindness at all.

13.7 The process of gaining knowledge and skills without being directly taught is called

    a. direct instruction.
    b. absorption.
    c. incidental teaching.
    d. confusion.

13.8 Mario is a student with deafblindness. Which communication method is he most likely to use?

    a. "hand over hand"
    b. ASL
    c. braille
    d. oral

13.9   Justin has a brain tumor. He is

a. not eligible to receive services as a student with TBI.
b. eligible for special education services as a student with TBI.
c. eligible for special education services as a student with TBI if the tumor causes him to lose consciousness.
d. eligible for special education services as a student with TBI only if an EEG shows brain damage.

13.10   Jameson's teachers are concerned about his hitting behavior. In order to identify the events that trigger his hitting, they should use

a. CBM.
b. functional behavioral assessment.
c. communication training.
d. social skills training.

Short Answer:

13.11   Compare and contrast the TASH and IDEA definitions of multiple-severe disabilities.

13.12   Describe functional assessments and what they should include.

13.13   Compare and contrast the IDEA and Baldwin definitions of deafblindness. Which one do you think is better suited for classroom teachers? Why?

13.14 Explain what you would do to make a student with deafblindness feel more comfortable in your class.

13.15 Explain when a functional behavioral assessment should be used and how it works.

Application:

13.16 You are the special education teacher for a 16-year-old student with deaf-blindness. What considerations need to be made for his education program at this time? What issues must you and the family consider for the future?

CHAPTER TEST ANSWERS

Chapter 1
1.1	B
1.2	D
1.3	B
1.4	D
1.5	A
1.6	D
1.7	D
1.8	D
1.9	D
1.10	C

Chapter 2
2.1	C
2.2	C
2.3	C
2.4	D
2.5	D
2.6	D
2.7	D
2.8	D
2.9	C
2.10	D

Chapter 3
3.1	D
3.2	A
3.3	D
3.4	C
3.5	D
3.6	D
3.7	C
3.8	D
3.9	C
3.10	C

Chapter 4
4.1	C
4.2	A
4.3	C
4.4	C
4.5	B
4.6	A
4.7	D
4.8	B
4.9	C
4.10	A

Chapter 5
5.1	A
5.2	B
5.3	B
5.4	C
5.5	B
5.6	B
5.7	C
5.8	D
5.9	B
5.10	C

Chapter 6
6.1	B
6.2	A
6.3	B
6.4	A
6.5	B
6.6	C
6.7	C
6.8	B
6.9	A
6.10	D

Chapter 7
7.1	B
7.2	D
7.3	D
7.4	C
7.5	A
7.6	A
7.7	B
7.8	C
7.9	B
7.10	A

Chapter 8
8.1	A
8.2	A
8.3	D
8.4	D
8.5	A
8.6	A
8.7	B
8.8	A
8.9	A
8.10	B

Chapter 9
9.1	A
9.2	A
9.3	B
9.4	C
9.5	D
9.6	C
9.7	D
9.8	A
9.9	C
9.10	A

Chapter 10
10.1	B
10.2	C
10.3	C
10.4	B
10.5	A
10.6	A
10.7	D
10.8	C
10.9	A
10.10	B

Chapter 11
11.1	A
11.2	D
11.3	B
11.4	A
11.5	D
11.6	A
11.7	C
11.8	A
11.9	B
11.10	D

Chapter 12
12.1	A
12.2	A
12.3	D
12.4	D
12.5	A
12.6	D
12.7	B
12.8	C
12.9	A
12.10	B

Chapter 13

12.1	A
12.2	C
12.3	B
12.4	D
12.5	D
12.6	C
12.7	C
12.8	A
12.9	A
12.10	B

PUZZLE ANSWER KEYS

PUZZLE ANSWER KEYS

CHAPTER 1

Cryptogram

Special education is individualized education that matches each child's specific needs with educational services.

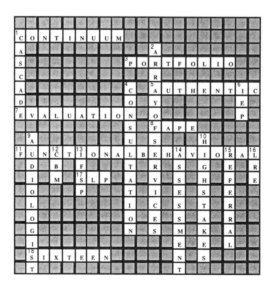

CHAPTER 2

CHAPTER 3

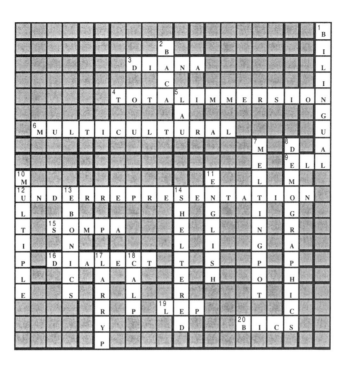

CHAPTER 4

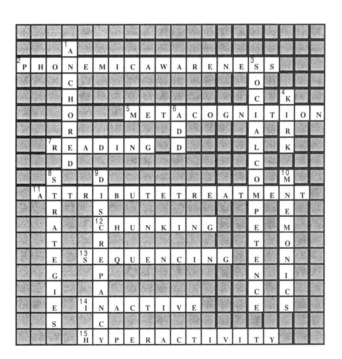

CHAPTER 4 (con't.)

	I	I	I	A	L	D	I	A	L	S		S										
	N	N	T	V	B	L	L	I	T	I	C	E		T	H		E		N	O	N	M	A	G
I	D	D	S	E	I	I	U	G	E	N	E	W	I	H	A	V	L	E	A	R	R	I	N	L
I	N	D	I	V	I	D	U	A	L	S		W	I	T	H		L	E	A	R	N	I	N	G
	D	I	S	A	B	I	L	I	T	I	E	S		H	A	V	E		N	O	R	M	A	L
	I	N	T	E	L	L	I	G	E	N	C	E												

CHAPTER 5

<u>Cryptogram</u>: Collaborative consultation is a shared responsibility. It requires teamwork!

A	R			M	U		T			O	A			
T	P	T	E	C	O	S	O	R	C	L	N	M	I	S
G	H	E	I	M	H	A	I	R	M	O	N	N	O	N
S	E	E	I	C	P	L	A	T	I	E	M	T	G	U	A
A	R	T	I	C	U	L	A	T	I	O	N			I	S	
T	H	E		M	O	S	T		C	O	M	M	O	N	
S	P	E	E	C	H		O	R		L	A	N	G	U	A
G	E		I	M	P	A	I	R	M	E	N	T		

CHAPTER 5 (con't.)

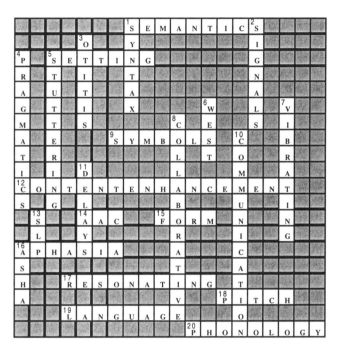

CHAPTER 6

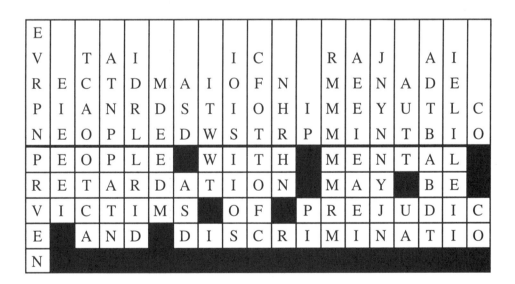

CHAPTER 6 (con't.)

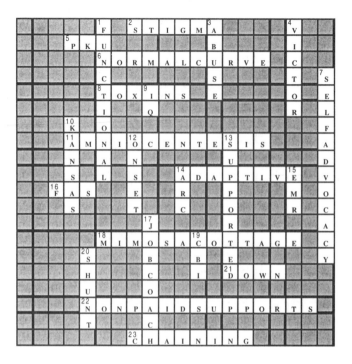

CHAPTER 7

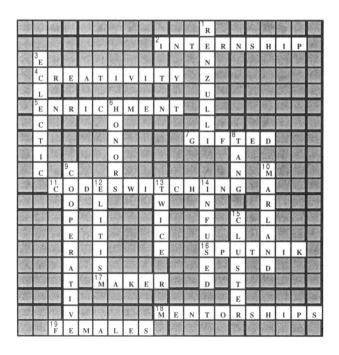

CHAPTER 8

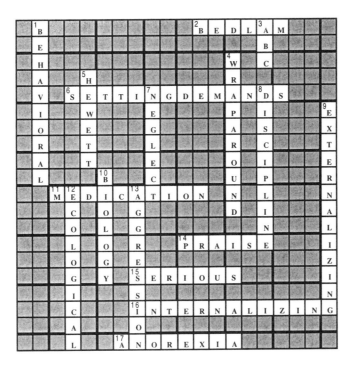

CHAPTER 9

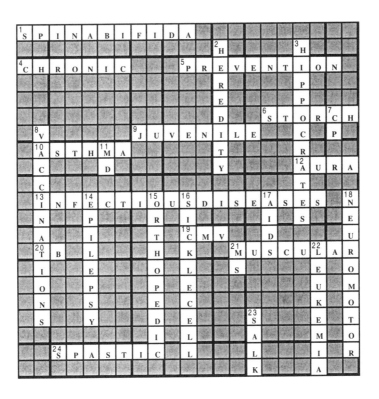

CHAPTER 10

Word Search

1. AUDIOGRAM: Grid used to display hearing abilities
2. AUDIOMETER: Instrument used for measuring hearing
3. AUDITORY NERVE: Carries messages from ear to brain
4. BILINGUAL: ASL is considered native language and English is second language
5. CONDUCTIVE: Hearing loss in outer or middle ear
6. CUED SPEECH: Hand signals that accompany difficult to see oral speech sounds
7. DEAFNESS: Inability to perceive sounds, with/without hearing aid
8. EARLY DETECTION: A key factor in prevention
9. HARD-OF-HEARING: Enough residual hearing to comprehend oral communication with a hearing   aid
10. INCUS: Anvil
11. INTERPRETERS: Related service providers; translators
12. MALLEUS: Hammer
13. ORAL ONLY: Method of communication using oral language only
14. OTITIS MEDIA: Middle ear infection; cause of hearing loss
15. POSTLINGUALLY: Hearing loss occurs after language development
16. RUBELLA: German measles; cause of hearing loss
17. SENSORINEURAL: Hearing loss in inner ear
18. STAPES: Stirrup

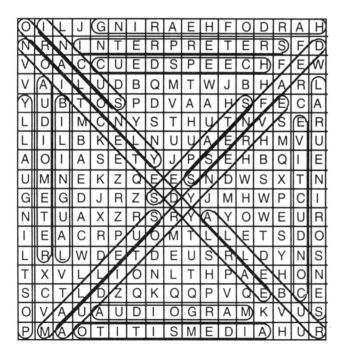

CHAPTER 10

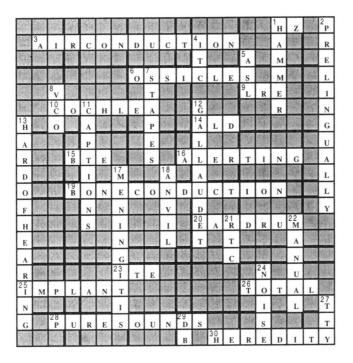

CHAPTER 11

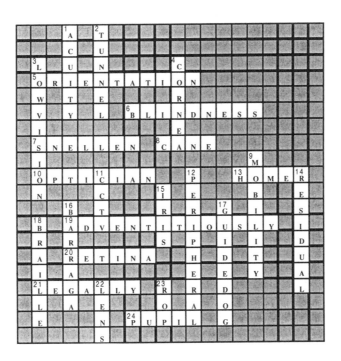

CHAPTER 12

C		S	L			E	R			G		U				
F		I	E		S	H	N		E	D	D	R		E	S	
O	E	R	P	E	T	I	E	V	P	I	S	H	C	T	D	
W	H	I	E	R	C	E	A	T	E	S	H	T	I	D	E	R	O
N	T	H	N	D	R	C	A	L	W	A	T	U	N	A	S	I	O
C	H	I	L	D	R	E	N		W	I	T	H		A	S	D	
W	E	R	E		S	E	R	V	E	D		U	N	D	E	R	
O	T	H	E	R		C	A	T	E	G	O	R	I	E	S		O
F		S	P	E	C	I	A	L		E	D	U	C	A	T	I	O
N		I	N		T	H	E		P	A	S	T					

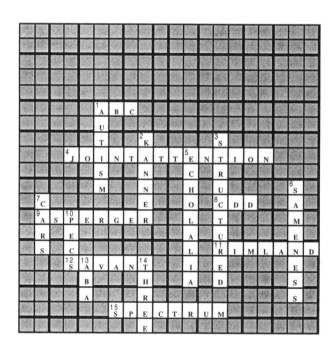

CHAPTER 13

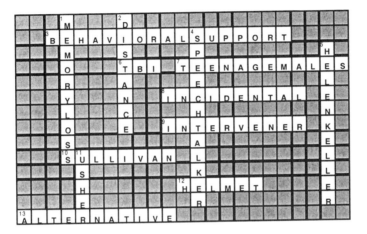

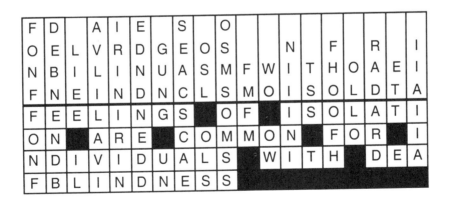

REFERENCES

Gallagher, W.F. (1988). Categorical services in the age of integration: Paradox or contradiction? *Journal of Visual Impairment and Blindness*, 82, 226-229.

Holmes, S.A. (1990, July 14). Rights bill for the disabled sent to Bush. *New York Times NATIONAL*, p. 7.

Matson, J.L. (Ed). (1994). *Autism in children and adults: Etiology, assessment, and intervention.* Pacific Grove, CA: Brooks/Cole Publishing Company.

Morrison, T. (1970). *The bluest eye.* New York: Washington Square Press.

Moss, P.C. (1990). *An autobiography: P. Buckley Moss: The people's artist.* Waynesboro, VA: Shenandoah Heritage Publishing Co.

Renzulli, J.S., & Reis, S.M. (1991). The reform movement and the quiet crisis in gifted education. *Gifted Child Quarterly*, 35, 26-35.

Smith, J.K., & Plimpton, G. (1993). *Chronicles of Courage.* New York: Random House.

Stallings, G., & Cook, S. (1997). *Another season: A coach's story of raising his exceptional son.* Boston: Little, Brown, and Co.

Sutherland, A.T. (1981). *Disabled we stand.* Cambridge, MA: Brookline Books.

Wright, M.H. (1999). *Sounds like home: Growing up Black and Deaf in the South.* Washington, DC: Gallaudet University Press.

NOTES

NOTES

NOTES

NOTES

NOTES

NOTES

NOTES

NOTES

NOTES

NOTES